The History of Economic Thought: A Concise Treatise for Business, Law, and Public Policy
Volume I

The History of Economic Thought: A Concise Treatise for Business, Law, and Public Policy
Volume I

From the Ancients Through Keynes

Professor Robert Ashford
Professor Stefan J. Padfield

BEP BUSINESS EXPERT PRESS

The History of Economic Thought: A Concise Treatise for Business, Law, and Public Policy Volume I: From the Ancients Through Keynes
Copyright © Business Expert Press, LLC, 2017.

First published in 2017 by
Business Expert Press, LLC
222 East 46th Street, New York, NY 10017
www.businessexpertpress.com

ISBN-13: 978-1-63157-069-8 (paperback)
ISBN-13: 978-1-63157-070-4 (e-book)

Business Expert Press Business Law Collection

Collection ISSN: 2333-6722 (print)
Collection ISSN: 2333-6730 (electronic)

Cover and interior design by S4Carlisle Publishing Services
Private Ltd., Chennai, India

First edition: 2017

10 9 8 7 6 5 4 3 2 1

Printed in the United States of America.

Dedication

I dedicate this history to
(1) my father, Theodore Askounes Ashford, who taught me how to think
rigorously and for myself; who taught me to always ask myself:
"How do you know?"
(2) my mother, Venette Askounes Ashford, who taught me compassion and
dedication for the least of these; and
(3) Julia Rowell, who lovingly cared for me from six weeks to six years old.

—Robert Ashford

I dedicate this history to
my brilliant wife and best friend, Dr. Maria E. Pagano.
Je t'aime.

—Stefan Padfield

Abstract

This two-volume concise treatise on the history of economic thought is accessibly written for readers interested in business, law, and public policy. Volume I and Chapters 11 and 12 of Volume II examine economics from its ancient origins through contemporary economics. Volume I, Chapters 1–10 discuss (1) the ancient Greek, Roman and Scholastic periods, (2) themercantile era, (3) Adam Smith, David Ricardo, Jeremy Bentham, John Stuart Mill and other classical economists, (5) socialist and other critics of classical economics including Karl Marx (6) founders of neoclassical economics, including Alfred Marshall and Leon Walras, (7) Keynesian economics and the rise and fall of Samuelson's Keynesian-neoclassical synthesis, and (8) other economic schools including Austrian, public choice, institutional, behavioral, and other heterodox schools. Volume II, Chapters 11 and 12 discuss economics following Keynes through contemporary economics and the Great Recession. Volume II, Chapters 13 and 14 provide an executive summary of the history and views and recommendations regarding its practical application.

Keywords

Adam Smith, Austerity, Austrian Economics, Binary Economics, Capacity Utilization, Economics, Economic Efficiency, Economic Growth, Economic Methods, Economic Theory, Environmental Economics, Evolutionary Economics, Feminist Economics, Full Employment, Georgist Economics, Great Depression, Great Recession, Heterodox Economics, Historicism, History of Economic Thought, Industrial Revolution, Innovation, Institutional Economics, Invisible Hand, Keynesian Economics, Louis Kelso, Monetary Theory, Neoclassical Economics, Price Theory, Rational Expectations, Socio-Economics, Socialist Economics, Stimulus, Unutilized Productive Capacity

Contents

Foreword

Our two-volume concise treatise on the history of economic thought is accessibly written for readers interested in business, law, and public policy. Volume I and Chapters 11 & 12 of Volume II examine economics from its ancient origins through contemporary economics. Volume I, Chapters 1–10 discuss (1) the ancient Greek, Roman and Scholastic periods, (2) the mercantile era, (3) Adam Smith, David Ricardo, Jeremy Bentham, John Stuart Mill and other classical economists, (5) socialist and other critics of classical economics including Karl Marx (6) founders of neoclassical economics, including Alfred Marshall and Leon Walras, (7) Keynesian economics and the rise and fall of Samuelson's Keynesian-neoclassical synthesis, and (8) other economic schools including Austrian, public choice, institutional, behavioral, and other heterodox schools. Volume II, Chapters 11 and 12 discuss economics following Keynes through contemporary economics and the Great Recession. Volume II, Chapters 13 and 14 provide a contemporary recapitulation and elaboration of the history and views and recommendations regarding its practical application.

Our history differs from other histories of economic thought by being shorter and in some ways more focused and comprehensive. Because it is written primarily for readers interested in business, law, and public policy, our treatment omits some developments frequently included in longer works written primarily for people with advanced training in economics. At the same time, our history discusses developments and principles important to business, law, and public policy regarding which other histories give little or no attention. Our exclusions and inclusions reflect judgments that not all developments that are important to theoreticians whose analyses rest on assumed conditions of perfect (or nearly perfect) competition are as important as other developments to people whose responsibilities and concerns require the application of economic principles under real-world imperfect conditions. One transcendent set of issues that divide both professional economists and others relates to what extent, why, and how economic agents and economies employ and fail to employ productive capacity efficiently and profitably and distribute income accordingly in exchange for productive inputs employed to produce goods and services in response to distributed demand. In addressing these and other issues, we have included numerous perspectives including some of our own. Recognizing that space limitations have required the omission of many other contributors to the history of economic thought that are worthy of consideration, we have provided numerous additional sources that readers may wish to investigate for additional analysis and other perspectives.

We also write with the recognition that economic phenomena and behavior are influenced not only by principles that apply regardless of what people believe but also by principles that are influenced by what people believe. Accordingly, an understanding of the history of economic thought is not only important in analyzing economic phenomena and behavior but may also be instrumental in influencing them.

We believe that readers wishing to gain helpful insights from the history of economic thought will find these volumes very rewarding. We welcome all feedback, positive and negative, from our readers.

Professor Robert Ashford
Bond, Schoeneck & King Distinguished Professor of Law
Syracuse University College of Law
rashford@law.syr.edu
ProfessorAshford@aol.com

Professor Stefan J. Padfield
University of Akron School of Law
spadfie@uakron.edu

CHAPTER 1

Introduction

It is often said that history is written by the victors, and thus important truths and perspectives of the vanquished are frequently excluded. But fortunately this is not as true in the history of economic thought. The only cost to the losers of economic theory is to be excluded from the continuing development of mainstream economics. Apart from this banishment (which some regard as a badge of honor), the losers are free to repeat and refine their thoughts and sharpen their critique of mainstream theory. Thus, the history of economic thought is replete with questions, challenges, and alternative views that facilitate a deeper, more comprehensive and practical understanding of mainstream theory and its limitations.

Consistent with these admonitions and observations, our goal in writing this book is to provide interested professionals, students, and other global citizens a concise introduction to the relevant breadth of economic theory in order to allow them to bring a healthy critical judgment to the myriad important economic issues of our day. This is particularly important given that economics is becoming seemingly ever more complex, controversial, and important to decisions related to business, law, and public policy.

This book differs from most books on the history of economic thought by being generally shorter but at the same time more focused and comprehensive in certain ways. To be concise, we have omitted discussion of some contributors to the history of economic thought and some contributions of included contributors which would otherwise be discussed in longer works.[1] Readers with some background in the history of economic thought may be shocked at some of the comparative space allotments (e.g., while Milton Friedman is discussed at length in various sections of this two-volume treatise, the section bearing his name consists of but a single paragraph while the following section on Paul Davidson covers five pages), but we believe readers will nonetheless find here everything they need to lay a solid foundation for their hopefully ongoing study of the history of economic thought.

At the same time, our book is also more focused and comprehensive because we have included discussion of contributors to contemporary economic thought and implications flowing from economic principles that are of special importance to business, law, and public policy and that are not generally discussed by other authors of similar works. Thus, although we highly recommend consulting a number of books and other sources on the history of economic thought, many of which have greatly influenced our work,[2] we believe this book will prove to be an especially valuable initial introduction for the reader with a particular interest in business, law, and/or public policy. The reader will likely quickly see that many of the historical events and debates we highlight in this book have direct relevance to current policy debates.

---

[1] Compare this work to reading R.B. Ekelund, Jr. and R.F. Hebert. 2013. *A History of Economic Theory & Method,* 6th ed., (Chicago: Waveland Press, Inc.) (hereinafter "Ekelund and Hebert") (733 pages) or T.G. Buchholz. 2007. *New Ideas from Dead Economists: An Introduction to Modern Economic Thought* (USA: Penguin) (368 pages), or listening to recorded lectures like T. Taylor's *Legacies of Great Economists* (7 hours and 24 minutes). Although we consider the concise nature of our work to be an asset, the longer sources listed in this footnote are all excellent and highly recommended for further reading, and we will routinely direct readers to specific portions of these works as well as those listed in the next footnote.

[2] Other related works of interest include: J.F. Bell. 1980. *A History of Economic Thought,* 2nd ed., (Huntington, New York: Robert E. Krieger Company) (hereinafter "Bell"); J.K. Galbraith. 1987. *Economics in Perspective: A Critical History* (Boston: Houghton Mifflin Company) (hereinafter "Galbraith"); H. Landreth and D.C. Colander. 1994. *History of Economic Thought,* 3rd ed., (Boston: Houghton Mifflin Company) (hereinafter "Landreth and Colander"); S. Pressman. 2013. *Fifty Major Economists,* 3rd ed., (New York: Routledge), p. 79.

So, what is economics? Not surprisingly it has been variously defined. One core definition that many economists would likely accept defines economics as the study of the production, distribution, and consumption of goods and services resulting from human choices among opportunities that are in some sense relatively scarce or mutually exclusive in order to achieve desired results. In a societal context, where people act both competitively and cooperatively, the relative scarcity arises from the fact that desires are frequently greater than the opportunities to satisfy them immediately, and thus one or more means are necessary to allocate the opportunities to satisfy those desires according to some priority. Historically, at least four social means of allocative priority can be identified: (1) brute force, (2) tradition, (3) authority (state or church), and (4) markets.[3] Although many people may believe that historically societies have moved sequentially from primary reliance on the first through the fourth means, a strong case can also be made for the proposition that even in the most modern economies all four forms of allocative means are presently operative. In modern times, the special appeal of markets is that they provide a means of voluntary exchange among producers and consumers that is widely assumed to be wealth-maximizing for the society as a whole.

As defined above, "economics" is broader than its widely acknowledged primary focus on the production, exchange, distribution, and consumption of goods and services in discrete markets like the supermarket, the real estate market, or the New York Stock Exchange. Because "goods and services" are broadly defined to include anything people might desire (including leisure) or, in other words, anything from which they might derive usefulness or "utility," some of the most celebrated and controversial contributions of economics may come from the application of economic analysis to implicit markets like, for example, marriage. Because much volitional human behavior involves choices that reflect the pursuit of desires (and therefore the expression of preferences reflecting trade-offs with foregone alternative courses of action), the scope of economic analysis is quite broad. Whether helpful understanding of human behavior regarding desires, in contexts

---

[3]Landreth and Colander, at p. 2.

4   THE HISTORY OF ECONOMIC THOUGHT, VOLUME I

both within and beyond discrete markets susceptible to meaningful quantification, is best achieved by way of the discipline of economics, psychology, sociology, anthropology, political science, history, biology, moral philosophy, religion, or some combination thereof is historically controversial both within and beyond the discipline of economics.

We conclude this introductory chapter with some important questions that are relevant to contemporary issues in law, business, and public policy and that may help to identify which contributors to the history of economic thought provide clarity, shed light, and/or fuel controversy. We suggest that you read these questions slowly and try to come up with your own answers to the questions, then return to them after you have finished reading this history to see how your answers may have changed and what you have learned.

- What motivates people? Different theorists will argue pain, pleasure, utility, indifference, altruism, or faith, to name a few. The famous psychologist Abraham Maslow postulated that people seek to satisfy a hierarchy of needs ranging from the physiological need for food, air, and water to "self-actualization."[4] This question is extremely important because when we rely on economists to help guide, for example, our governmental policy making, we are assuming they can to some meaningful extent predict how people will respond to various conditions, which requires knowing what motivates people.
- What are the causes of per-capita growth (i.e., per-capita increases in production)?
- What effect does distribution have on growth?
- Which causes of growth are comprehended by economic theory (endogenous) and which causes are external to economic theory (exogenous)?[5]

---

[4]M.H. Abraham. 1943. "A theory of human motivation," *Psychological Review* 50, no. 4, pp. 370–96 (identifying physiological safety, love and belonging, esteem, and self-actualization).

[5]An example of a factor determining long-run growth that may be considered exogenous to standard economic models is unexpected technological progress. The more economic growth that is attributed to such exogenous factors, the less predictive power can be ascribed to the economic models.

- Do economies gravitate toward equilibrium (as Adam Smith and most modern economists assume), or is the process evolutionary? In other words, are economic phenomena Newtonian or Darwinian? Arguably on the Darwinian side, the ancient Greek philosopher Heraclitus is said to have proclaimed: "You never step into the same river twice."[6]
- Is economics more a natural science or social science?
- What is the relation between efficiency and growth?
- To what extent are future economic phenomena determined by (or predictable based on) the past? In other words, what economic phenomena are ergodic or nonergodic?[7]
- What is unutilized capacity? In what context, if any, does it exist?
- What are the determinants of value and price?
- What is included within "capital?" What are the differences between real and financial capital? What determines its earning capacity, rate of return, and price? What is its relation to the interest rate?
- To what extent are the costs of production (present and future) reflected in market prices? (This question raises the problem of externalities.)
- Does monetary policy matter in the short and long run? Is money "neutral"?
- How do opportunity costs differ from other (expensed) costs?
- Does economics have a normative component?
- What is the relation of regulation to property, autonomy, efficiency, and growth?
- What is the relation between economics and democracy?
- What is the theory of the second best?

---

[6]As quoted in Plato, *Cratylus,* 402a.

[7]The assertion that future economic developments can be predicted on the basis of past and present experiences may be described as the "ergodic axiom." The harder it is to make such predictions, the more the economy may be described as nonergodic.

Although we may not directly answer every one of these questions, we may at least provide a sufficient grounding in the history of economic thought to allow readers to begin to generate answers on their own. As suggested above, it would likely be a useful exercise to return to these questions once the reader has completed this history.

CHAPTER 2

Overview of the History of Economic Thought from the Ancients Through Keynes

In this chapter, we will provide a brief overview of the material set forth in more detail in the remainder of this volume. Hopefully, this will provide the reader with a useful outline that will make it easier to digest the subsequent chapters. However, reading this overview should in no way be understood to serve as a replacement for reading the remainder of the book, as space limitations have led to a number of important ideas and theorists being left to the pages following this overview.

The roots of modern economics can be found in the Ancients, including Xenophon (c. 430–354 BC), Plato (c. 427–347 BC), Aristotle (384–322 BC), Heraclitus (c. 535–475 BC), Zeno (c. 490–430 BC), and the Romans. The word "economics" itself arguably comes from Xenophon's *Oeconomicus* (c. 360 BC). Plato identified specialization and the division of labor as leading to increased efficiency and productivity; but to achieve the greatest social welfare, he did not believe markets were capable of complete self-regulation. He was also concerned about the corruption of individuals via an unbridled pursuit of profit. Furthermore, in his *Republic*, Plato expressed concerns about the divisiveness and discord engendered by private property. In contrast, Aristotle took the view that "It is clearly better that property should be private" (*Politics* Book II, Part V). At the same time, Aristotle worried that encouraging the accumulation of money in order to make more money would foster unbridled self-interest in a way that would lead to inequality and distributive injustice.[1] In addition, the tension between Heraclitus's dynamic view of the world and Zeno's static view set the stage for a debate that continues to the present day. Essentially, the question is whether it is more appropriate to view economic life as governed by fixed laws akin to the laws of Newtonian physics or changing phenomena more akin to evolutionary Darwinism. Finally, by way of its codification of principles reflected in the law of private property, contracting, and the corporation as an independent entity distinct from its investors and agents, the Roman contribution to the foundations of economic theory is enormous.

Next we come to the Scholastics. With the fall of the Roman Empire, the Catholic Church became the primary source of social authority in most of Europe. Economic activity was highly localized, but the authority of the Church pervaded economic thinking throughout the domain of its influence. Albert Magnus (c. 1206–1280) aligned value-in-exchange with cost-of-production (labor and expenses), which, as we shall see, laid the foundation that was to be built upon for generations. Coming at the problem of value from another perspective, Thomas Aquinas (c. 1225–1274) focused on demand, arguing that price varies with desire, and thus need/want becomes another regulator of value. Aquinas, following in the footsteps of the Greeks, also struggled with the notion of "just price."

In the history of economic thought, the period from roughly 1450 through 1750 is known as the Mercantile period. Thus, Mercantilism can be understood as a bridge between feudalism and capitalism, which is tied to the rise of the defense of greater individual liberty in the eighteenth century, and the Industrial Revolution in the nineteenth century. Banks and currency exchanges appeared, first in Italy and then in northern Europe, and became a regular feature of commercial activity. The merchant emerged from the feudal shadows to become a distinctive figure with increasing social acceptance, prestige, and power. With the rise of

---

[1]For a modern take on inequality, see generally T. Piketty. 2014. *Capital in the Twenty First Century* (Cambridge: Belknap). *Cf.* P. Krugman. May, 2014. "Why We're in a New Gilded Age," *The New York Review of Books* (describing Piketty's book as resulting in "a revolution in our understanding of long-term trends in inequality"), *available at* http://www.nybooks.com/articles/2014/05/08/thomas-piketty-new-gilded-age/.

the nation-state came a close association of state interest and merchant interest. Unlike earlier times, when economics was the work of philosophers, in the mercantile world economic analysis was primarily the product of statesmen, civil servants, and business leaders. Although practiced with considerable variation by virtually every European nation-state of the time, the mercantilists were united in the goal of making and maintaining a strong nation-state by strengthening its political and economic power. In Mercantilism, one can also see a shift from the Scholastic focus on justice and salvation to a more secular focus on wealth and power. Nevertheless, throughout most of the period Mercantilism shared the earlier Platonic assumption that, contrary to Adam Smith's subsequent analysis, there existed a fundamental conflict between the pursuit of private interests (private wealth maximization) and the welfare of the society as a whole. Unlike Smith and the market economists that followed him, the early mercantilists did not see win–win benefits flowing from free trade, but rather saw trade as a zero-sum game.

One doctrinal principle of Mercantilism remains a vital issue of controversy today: the question of the neutrality or non-neutrality of money. A tenet of Mercantilism was that changes in the supply of money lead to changes in the real output of the economy. In contrast, Adam Smith and the other classical economists believed that the level of economic activity depends on factors such as the quantity and quality of labor, natural resources, capital goods, technological advances, and institutional structure. Any changes in the quantity of money, they maintained, would affect neither the long-run level of output nor growth, but only the level of prices. As will be discussed later, in the twentieth century, John Maynard Keynes essentially sided with the mercantilist by declaring that by reason of a liquidity preference, money is never neutral in either the short or the long run.[2]

The Physiocrats, who formed the final leg of the journey to Adam Smith and the dawn of capitalism, published most of their works between

---

[2] *See generally*, Liquidity Preference. 1968. *Encyclopedia.com* (noting that Keynes identified three motives for demanding money: to facilitate ordinary transactions, hedging, and speculation), *available at* http://www.encyclopedia.com/doc/1G2-3045000720 .html.

1756 and 1778. The Physiocrats sought to address the economic woes of France by coming to understand economic growth as part of an organic, natural system ("Physiocracy" means "rule of nature"). According to the Physiocrats, once the unnatural and unhealthy burdens of excessive taxation and trade restrictions were lifted, the circulation of income and expenditures would be restored and France's economy could start to head back in the right direction. However, the Physiocrats' preference for agriculture lent credence to the uniqueness of land and, thereby, the nobility that owned it. Thus, the Physiocrats have been accused of trying to mount a return to feudalism rather than the developing industrialization that led to capitalism.

Before 1776, a number of writers offered significant insights into the dynamics of economic systems and the flawed analyses and policies of the early Mercantilists and Physiocrats, but none was able to offer a comprehensive systemic analysis that caught the widespread attention of their contemporaries. It was Adam Smith who achieved relatively widespread contemporary recognition of the analytical foundation established in *The Wealth of Nations*—a recognition that earned Smith almost universal acceptance as the father of political economy and modern economics. The period between 1776 and 1870, beginning with publication of Adam Smith's *The Wealth of Nations*, and spanning the contributions of Jeremy Bentham (1748–1832), David Ricardo (1772–1823), Robert Malthus (1766–1834), and John Stuart Mill (1806–1873), was so rich in terms of building the structure we now know as economics that it is referred to as the classical period.

Smith was already highly regarded before publishing *The Wealth of Nations*, owing to his 1759 work, *The Theory of Moral Sentiments*, in which he argued that man could act morally, despite being a fundamentally selfish creature, because he was capable of sympathizing with his fellow man. A great deal of Smith's political economy was rooted in a belief in natural law, which aligned Smith with a *laissez-faire* approach to government, since any enacted positive law could by definition be deemed inferior to the law of nature. Smith famously characterized this superiority of natural law as an "invisible hand" both in *The Theory of Moral Sentiments* and in *The Wealth of Nations*. However, while Smith arguably believed in a natural identity of interest, such that order and harmony would arise naturally where individuals are free to pursue their self-interest, Bentham believed an artificial identity of interest was required for order, and that it was the legislature's job to align the interests of individuals in such a way as to, for example, minimize the incidence of crime.

In *An Essay on the Principle of Population*, Thomas Robert Malthus responded to some of the utopian optimism of his day by pointing out that the combination of scarcity of resources (particularly food) and overpopulation would inevitably thwart any march to utopia—in fact, it would result in a subsistence economy. David Ricardo advanced the notion of a stationary equilibrium state, which added to Malthus's predictions regarding wages ultimately resting at subsistence levels due to the pressure of incessant population growth by noting that profits also would be squeezed—particularly by the increasing rent payments required to expand production growth—to a point just slightly above zero.

John Stuart Mill is perhaps best known for his works *On Liberty* (1859) and *Utilitarianism* (1863), but it is his *Principles of Political Economy* (1848) that primarily concerns us here. Mill distinguished between laws of production, which may be fixed and subject to pure economic analysis, and laws of distribution, which are ultimately malleable and subject to a variety of perspectives. Mill also was very willing to accept government interference in a capitalist economy wherever it might serve some greater good rather than deferring to strict *laissez-faire* policies. He noted a number of areas, like consumer protection, preservation of the environment, and public utility regulation, which allowed for government intervention. Although Mill did not abandon the deductive aspects of a belief in natural law so central to Adam Smith, he did aspire to increase the extent to which inductive empiricism was relied upon in economics. Mill also challenged the notion of a fixed pool of funds being available for wages (the wages-fund doctrine) by arguing that capitalists could expand the pool of capital available for wages by reducing the amount they spent on themselves for nonessential goods.

The Industrial Revolution has had an immense impact on the way goods (and services) are produced, distributed, and consumed in every major world economy. Its beginning can be dated to as early as the Gutenberg Press (1440) but more often is dated from around 1760–1830. Fixing an endpoint is problematic in principle. Although many people describe the contemporary economy as "post-industrial," there is reason to question whether an advance in computer technology that vastly increases total output per unit of labor input is significantly different in its most important economic effects from nineteenth-century advances in looms, harvesters, steel making, and electrical power.[3]

In terms of a massive increase in per-capita production and productive capacity, the Industrial Revolution was obviously a boon to both England and the world in many ways. But it also brought with it urban decay and overcrowding, abusive labor conditions, and heightened awareness of income disparities between the rich and poor. The criticisms and calls for reform were a direct challenge to classical economics because it was associated with the Industrial Revolution as a cause and because it advanced theories that posited reform as futile. Discomfort with the unequal manner in which the wealth being created by the Industrial Revolution was being distributed, as well as the squalid conditions the lower-class men, women, and children labored in, led to the rise of socialism. There were also concerns expressed regarding the psychological toll of the materialism and consumerism that capitalism was perceived to foster.

Most of the reformers were seeking various forms of voluntary change, but Karl Marx (1818–1883) considered these approaches utopian. Marx agreed with Adam Smith that specialization and the division of labor were key drivers to increased productivity, but he disagreed with Smith by concluding that this division of labor would ultimately lead to greater and greater conflict between individuals. Marx was also a critic of private property because it allowed for the accumulation of wealth in the hands

---

[3] *But cf.* T. Alloway. July, 2016. "A 164-Year-Old Idea Helps Explain the Huge Changes Sweeping the World's Workforce," *Bloomberg.com* (noting that some analysts argue the third industrial revolution is threatening to replace human labor completely), *available at* http://www.bloomberg.com/news/articles/2016-07-20/a-164-year-old -idea-helps-explain-the-huge-changes-sweeping-the-world-s-workforce.   The second industrial revolution is typically cited as spanning roughly 1870–1914 and is commonly referred to as the Technological Revolution.   *Cf.* I. Wladawsky-Berger. February, 2016. "Preparing for the Fourth Industrial Revolution," *Blogs.wsj.com* (citing breakthroughs in fields from artificial intelligence to nanotechnology as pointing to a fourth industrial revolution), *available at* http://blogs.wsj.com/cio/2016/02/26 /preparing-for-the-fourth-industrial-revolution/.

of a few at the expense of the many. He pointed out the inherent contradiction in Political Economy whereby the laborer is "alienated" from what he or she produces, and he argued that the social institutions that thrive in this capitalist system do so because they are effective in getting the masses to conform. Marx made a number of predictions regarding capitalism, all of which he argued would lead ultimately to revolution.

Neoclassical economics, with its microeconomic focus on the firm and/or individual as opposed to the classical macroeconomic focus on the economy as a whole, as well as its rejection of purely objective formulations of value (allowing for the inclusion of subjectivity), together with its comfort with both the growing use of mathematical modeling and criticism of overdependence on these models, rose out of what was left of classical economics after it had been battered by Mill's rejection of the wages-fund doctrine, Marx's broadsides against the exploitation and alienation created by the capitalism that rested on classical economics, and the inability of classical economics to respond to the pressing issues of the day, many of which revolved around the rise of railroads as discrete economic actors. Various commentators have argued that the essence of neoclassical economics resides in marginalism, the subjective theory of utility, and/or the static analysis of resource allocation efficiency. Alfred Marshall (1842–1924) and Leon Walras (1834–1910) have been referred to as the cofounders of modern neoclassical economics.

Thorstein Veblen (1857–1929) is known as the founder of "institutional economics."[4] Institutionalism has been identified as the only widely recognized, uniquely American school of economics, though Veblen was to at least some extent influenced by the British Historicists. Institutionalism pushed back against the static theorizing of neoclassical economic analysis, advancing a more "Darwinian" view, and is considered part of the heterodox strand of economic thought. Veblen was part of an American culture of pragmatism, which maintained a skeptical view of the highly theoretical perspectives of the classical and neoclassical forms of economic

---

[4]The Reverend Richard Jones is also sometimes regarded as the first institutionalist for his 1831 publication, *An Essay on the Distribution of Wealth and on the Sources of Taxation*, which was critical of Ricardian analysis for not taking a global enough view of economics.

analysis emanating from Europe. He challenged the neoclassical notion of humans as rational, wealth-maximizing actors, describing the actors in his *Theory of the Leisure Class* as driven by an irrational desire for social status. He described a growing separation of finance and production, manifesting in the desire to make money trumping the desire to produce goods, and he anticipated regulatory capture by business interests.

With John Maynard Keynes (1883–1946), we will see a shift from microeconomic analysis back to the macroeconomics of classical economic analysis. Significantly, Keynes rejected the full-employment promise of Walrasian general equilibrium theory in its entirety, both in the short and the long run. Keynes also rejected the "money-neutrality" principle. According to Keynes, by reason of a savers' preference for liquidity, money is never neutral. This rejection leads to a fundamentally different understanding of another one of the bedrock theories of classical economic thought: the quantity theory of money. Keynes argued that as long as an economy is operating at less than full capacity, economic stimulus by way of increasing the money supply and deficit spending will not cause inflation, and economic circumstances could exist wherein the benefits of pumping money into the economy greatly outweigh the risk of inflation. He also argued for active use of fiscal tools (i.e., taxing, and spending) to generate the aggregate demand necessary to maximize employment.

Keynes's views were not accepted in economics departments by the then-prevailing neoclassical orthodoxy. It was only in the late 1940s, after Paul Samuelson modified Keynes's approach to harmonize it with Walrasian principles in the long run (which Keynes rejected), that a modified presentation of his approach was accepted as suitable for teaching succeeding generations of economists. This so-called neoclassical Keynesian synthesis held dominant sway over the Western world from the 1930s to the 1960s. Beginning in the 1970s, however, rapid inflation led to a resurgence of monetarism, which favored giving markets time to clear issues like unemployment rather than risking inflation via governmental deficit spending designed to create jobs. The debate continues to the modern day, and we can see it in action particularly around the post-crisis austerity movements in Europe.

Finally, additional schools of economic thought, including Austrian Economics, Public Choice Theory, Behavioral Economics, Happiness Theory, and Institutional Economics, will be covered. We hope you will enjoy this concise treatise on the history of economic thought.

CHAPTER 3

Preclassical Economics

The Ancients and Scholastics, Mercantilism, Physiocracy, and Other Classical Forerunners

Modern economics traces its roots to Adam Smith, who published his famous *An Inquiry into the Nature and Causes of the Wealth of Nations* in 1776. In order to better understand the economic analysis of Adam Smith, and the impact he had on the study of economics, it is important to understand some of the intellectual history that led up to his foundational, groundbreaking *Wealth of Nations*. Much of this history can be summed up as being covered by the Western natural law tradition spanning from antiquity, through feudalism, and up to the merchant capitalism of the mercantilists. While defining "natural law" can be complicated, with competing definitions at times appearing downright contradictory, we use it here to mean simply a belief that human behavior is subject to unseen, preexisting principles (widely regarded as "laws") of human nature, which can be discovered through observation and the application of reason. For example, and as we will discuss in more detail below, Adam Smith advanced the notion that markets are naturally self-regulating in ways that increase desired wealth creation and distribution. One can readily conjure up the myriad questions that such a proposition presents: What are the necessary preconditions for markets to self-regulate in ways that maximize societal well-being? How does one determine the extent to which those conditions are met? Inasmuch as Smith saw the need for regulation to protect private property, what regulation is needed to meet those preconditions? How do we measure the value exchanged within, and created by, self-regulating markets in order to assess whether they maximize societal well-being? And so on. While we will have more time to dig into these questions more deeply, what follows is a brief examination of some of the relevant thinkers and ideas leading up to Adam Smith.

The Ancients

The word "economics" arguably comes from Xenophon's *Oeconomicus* (c. 360 BC) wherein he discussed efficient management in both private and public affairs. A decorated soldier and student of Socrates, Xenophon demonstrated a rough understanding of a number of contemporary economic concepts, including the importance of (1) maximizing wealth, efficiency, and beneficial resource allocation (i.e., maximizing surplus); (2) good individual decision making as the primary cause of maximizing surplus (via management and entrepreneurship); (3) labor specialization; (4) economies of scale (favoring larger over smaller cities); (5) diminishing marginal utility ("the greater the number of superfluous dishes set before a man, the sooner a feeling of repletion comes over him"[1]); and (6) the subjectivity and relativity of value ("The same things are wealth or not wealth, according as one understands or does not understand how to use them. A flute . . . is wealth to one . . . competent to play it, but to an incompetent person . . . no better than useless stones . . . unless he sells it."[2]).

Plato (c. 427–347 BC) identified specialization and the division of labor as leading to increased efficiency and productivity, spurring individuals to congregate in cities to exchange goods and services in markets using money as a token of exchange—all modern economic concepts. However, to achieve the greatest social welfare, he did not believe markets were capable of complete self-regulation. Rather, he believed that, like the state, markets require administrative control. Plato was also concerned about the corruption of individuals via an unbridled pursuit of profit, and argued for an authoritarian regime

---

[1] E.C. Marchant. *Scripta Minora* (London: William Heinemann Ltd), p. 9, available at https://ryanfb.github.io/loebolus-data/L183.pdf.

[2] *Oeconomicus*, 1.10, available at http://www.perseus.tufts.edu/hopper/text?doc=Perseus%3Atext%3A1999.01.0212%3Atext%3DEc.%3Achapter%3D1.

managed by a ruling class of "guardians" devoid of interests in private property to govern with the aim of justice for all.

Plato had little faith in democracy, predicting that turning statesmanship over to the masses would devolve into tyranny. Better, he thought, to aspire to groom a few exceptional men devoid of interest in private gain who could therefore govern fairly for the good of the entire society. This lack of faith in the ability of individuals to manage their affairs in ways consistent with the good of society stands in stark contrast to Adam Smith's later belief in the benefits of largely unregulated markets.[3]

One very basic line of demarcation in economics lies between those who favor strong private property rights, along with limited government intervention when it comes to the private individual's use and growth of that property, versus those who favor a more active role for government when it comes to directing the use of private property, as well as the distribution of the wealth created by the use of that property. In *Republic*, Plato expressed concerns about the divisiveness and discord engendered by private property:

"Do we know of any greater evil for a state than the thing that distracts it and makes it many instead of one, or a greater good than that which binds it together and makes it one?"

"We do not."

"Is not, then, the community of pleasure and pain the tie that binds, when, so far as may be, all the citizens rejoice and grieve alike at the same births and deaths?"

"By all means," he said.

"But the individualization of these feelings is a dissolvent, when some grieve exceedingly and others rejoice at the same happenings to the city and its inhabitants?"

---

[3]Alternatively, one might argue that Plato's idealized role-based society may be consistent with Smith's invisible hand if one believes individuals will naturally fall into distinct roles that match their particular strengths and weaknesses. *Cf.* T. Strawn. Winter/Spring, 2013. "Book Review: A History of Homo Economicus: The Nature of the Moral in Economic Theory By David Wilson and William Dixon," *Moral Cents: The Journal of Ethics in Finance*, pp.45–48.

"And the chief cause of this is when the citizens do not utter in unison such words as 'mine' and 'not mine' . . . ."[4]

Nevertheless, in his ideal *Republic*, Plato did not deny the institution of private property to any class but to the guardians, who were to lead an ascetic life without property beyond the bare essentials.[5] Nor did he deny the citizens of the *Republic* the institution of trade via the market and the use of money but, revealing a lack of faith in self-regulatory markets, he insisted on fiat money and a strong state regulatory role to prevent usury and promote just prices and distribution.

In contrast, Aristotle (c. 384–322 BC) took the view that, "It is clearly better that property should be private":

> Property should be in a certain sense common, but, as a general rule, private; for, when everyone has a distinct interest, men will not complain of one another, and they will make more progress, because every one will be attending to his own business. . . . It is clearly better that property should be private, but the use of it common; and the special business of the legislator is to create in men this benevolent disposition. . . . And further, there is the greatest pleasure in doing a kindness or service to friends or guests or companions, which can only be rendered when a man has private property. These advantages are lost by excessive unification of the state.[6]

In addition to his views on private property Aristotle made early contributions to the economic understanding of wealth, value, and money (which was in common use in Athens well before the time of Plato). According to Aristotle, "wealth may be defined as a number of instruments to be used in a household or a state" for the purpose of realizing

---

[4] *Plat. Rep.* 5.462.
[5] Of the rulers, Plato wrote: "[S]hould they ever acquire homes or lands or moneys of their own, they will become good house keepers and husbandmen instead of guardians, enemies and tyrants instead of allies of the other citizens . . . ." *Republic.*
[6] *Politics* Book II, Part V.

the "good life."[7] Regarding value, Aristotle distinguished use-value and exchange-value.[8] Regarding money, in his *Ethics*, with a remarkably advanced understanding, he identifies three functions: (1) "a sort of medium or mean" of exchange, (2) a store of value, and (3) "a standard upon which the world agrees" (i.e., unit of measure).[9]

Although Aristotle appears to have been more in line than Plato with modern mainstream economic views regarding the benefits of private property, he did espouse views of trade and interest that run counter to many modern views. He favored trade as just and natural so long as it was based on an equality of wants.[10] Such trade involves the creation of goods via the skillful management of land and house, and the natural exchange of such goods for goods naturally created by another.[11] However, Aristotle opposed retail trade because it did not arise naturally from the normal activities of daily living.[12] As defined, the amount of wealth to be gained by producer trade was inherently limited to the productive capacity of well-managed households, whereas the amount that can be amassed by retail trade is unlimited.

However, Aristotle thought usury (i.e., charging interest) the most unnatural, and therefore worst, means of gaining wealth because it "makes a gain out of money itself, and not from the natural objects of it."[13] Thus, "money was intended to be used in exchange,

---

[7]*See* J.F. Bell. 1980. *A History of Economic Thought,* 2nd ed., (Huntington, New York: Robert E. Krieger Publishing Company), pp. 23–24 (quoting Aristotle).

[8]*See id.*

[9]*See id.* at pp. 24–25 (quoting Aristotle).

[10]*See* Aristotle. *Nicomachean Ethics* ("If, then, first there is proportionate equality of goods, and then reciprocal action takes place, the result we mention will be effected. If not, the bargain is not equal, and does not hold . . . ."), *available at* http://people .bu.edu/wwildman/courses/wphil/readings/wphil_rdg09_nichomacheanethics _entire.htm.

[11]*See* J.F. Bell. 1980. *A History of Economic Thought,* 2d ed., (Huntington, New York: Robert E. Krieger Publishing Company), pp. 23–24.

[12]*See id.*

[13]*See id.* (quoting Aristotle).

but not to increase at interest."[14] Aristotle worried that encouraging the accumulation of money in order to make more money would foster unbridled self-interest in a way that would lead to inequality and distributive injustice. Thus, although Plato and Aristotle had different views on private property, they apparently shared a concern for the adverse social consequences that might result from the concentration of great wealth (well beyond the needs of consumption) into private hands.

Before moving on from our brief review of some of the important economic discussions surviving in the writings of classical Greece, we pause to note one other issue that was raised then, and which continues to divide thinkers today: Heraclitus's dynamic view of the world versus Zeno's static view. In one of the "Method Squabbles" entries in their highly regarded textbook on the history of economic thought, Ekelund and Hebert describe the dynamic view as one that identifies the "ever-fluctuating" surface phenomena of existence as the primary source of knowledge about the world, while the static view posits an underlying unchanging reality that must be discovered to understand the world. [15] Although there are likely multiple ways of dissecting the debate, in their entry Ekelund and Hebert end up aligning the static view with natural law, enlightenment determinism, Adam Smith's invisible hand, and much of neoclassical economic doctrine.[16] On the other hand, the dynamic view is aligned with evolutionary Darwinism, as well as the institutional economics of Thorstein Veblen (1857–1929) and the evolutionary economics of Joseph Schumpeter (1883–1950).[17] Although the implications for economic theory that flow from the differences between the static and dynamic views may seem unfamiliar to the reader, rest assured that they will continue to be fleshed out throughout the course of this book, and it is sufficient for now to just file the distinction away for future use.

---

[14]*See id.* (quoting Aristotle).

[15]*See* Ekelund and Hebert, pp. 19–20.

[16]*See id.*

[17]*See id.*

Notwithstanding the vast, pervasive, and long-lasting dominance of the Roman Empire in Europe, the Middle East, and Northern Africa, historians of economic thought are in seemingly unanimous agreement that Roman philosophers and scholars left little or no surviving contributions to economic thought. Nevertheless, by way of its codification of principles reflected in the law of private property,[18] contracting, and the corporation as an independent entity distinct from its investors and agents, the Roman contribution to the foundations of economic theory is enormous. Without the legal infrastructure needed to support the financing and operation of corporations, as well as enabling them to contract, own assets, and conduct ordinary business as entities distinct from the shareholder-investors, modern economies would not exist in their present form. It seems fair to say that the social behavior recognized as "economic" in nature and the principles governing it are ultimately dependent on enforceable legal rights and obligations.

The Scholastics

During the Scholastic period of medieval Europe,[19] the issues of value and price continued to be important points of focus. In most of Europe the Catholic Church became the primary source of social authority with the fall of the Roman Empire. Economic activity was highly localized, but the authority of the Church pervaded economic thinking throughout the domain of its influence. As noted earlier, value is extremely important in economics whether one espouses self-regulating markets, regulated markets, or other means for determining price. The economic arguments in favor of self-regulating markets turn on the degree to which they promote the creation of greater value for individuals and society beyond that possible via alternative means such as various forms of regulation or nonmarket planning. Thus, both for those who advocate

---

[18] *See generally*, N.M. Mustapha. 2009. *Economics: The Historical, Religious & Contemporary Perspectives: A Treatise* (Central Milton Keynes: AuthorHouse), p. 10.

[19] For a discussion of important "Roman and Early Christian Contributions," "Chinese Economics in the First Millennium," and "Medieval Arab-Islamic Economics," see Ekelund and Hebert at pp. 21–27.

for free markets and those who question their superiority, there must be a valid way of assigning and measuring value beyond the market price itself, lest the assertion that market price reflects value becomes tautological. Unfortunately, there is no single widely accepted alternative way of assigning and measuring value.

The scholastic period focused largely on the moral dimensions of just price-setting by those who provided goods and services. In the present-day context, such moral dimensions are likely to be perceived as merely advisory or hortatory, but in medieval times, when the power of the Church over secular life was substantial, moral prescription carried with it a compulsory aspect and for the faithful the threat of damnation. To this end, Albert Magnus (c. 1206–1280) aligned value-in-exchange with cost-of-production (labor and expenses), which, as we shall see, laid a foundation that was to be built upon for generations. The rationale was that if a producer could not cover costs via exchange, production resources would be diverted elsewhere. The formulation contained notions of price as indicating an equilibrium value (more on this later) and cost as a regulator of value.

Coming at the problem of value from another perspective, Thomas Aquinas (c. 1225–1274) focused on demand, arguing that price varies with desire, and thus need/want becomes another regulator of value.[20] Distilling the relevant components of an appropriate measure of demand (e.g., aggregate versus individual, utility versus unmitigated desire) continued to be debated for a long time after Aquinas.

---

[20]The reader is cautioned to keep in mind that when economists refer to demand or desire, they are often best understood as limiting their discussion to demands or desires that the relevant consumer-to-be can pay for in some way. The implications of this shorthand nomenclature for discussions about the social optimality of free market exchange are to a great extent beyond the scope of this book. *See generally*, Commonwealth Department of the Environment, Sport and Territories, Commonwealth Department of Finance, and Resource Assessment Commission. 1995. *Techniques to Value Environmental Resources: an Introductory Handbook* (Canberra: Australian Government Publishing Service) (noting in *Chapter 2: The role of economics: Limitations of monetary valuation* that basing value on ability to pay without regard to distribution of wealth can be expected to result in the preferences of wealthy people being favored).

Aquinas, following in the footsteps of the Greeks, also struggled with the notion of "just price":

> [W]e may speak of buying and selling, considered as accidentally tending to the advantage of one party, and to the disadvantage of the other: for instance, when a man has great need of a certain thing, while another man will suffer if he be without it. On such a case the just price will depend not only on the thing sold, but on the loss which the sale brings on the seller. And thus it will be lawful to sell a thing for more than it is worth in itself, though the price paid be not more than it is worth to the owner. Yet if the one man derive a great advantage by becoming possessed of the other man's property, and the seller be not at a loss through being without that thing, the latter ought not to raise the price, because the advantage accruing to the buyer, is not due to the seller, but to a circumstance affecting the buyer. Now no man should sell what is not his, though he may charge for the loss he suffers. (Summa Theologica, Secunda Secundae Partis, Article I, Question 77)

However, the concept of just price has been heavily criticized by a number of modern economists, with many arguing that there is no need to speculate about it when competitive markets can be relied upon to regulate price.

In addition to "just price," the issue of interest, or "usury," was one of the main economic topics discussed by the Scholastics during the Middle Ages, again tracking the concerns of the Ancients. Usury can be generally understood as the act of a lender charging a fee for the use of loaned money (in other words, full repayment of the loan will consist of the return of the amount borrowed plus an amount typically consisting of a percentage of the amount borrowed adjusted for the time to repayment and the risk of default, which is typically referred to as "interest"). A general prohibition of usury can be traced as far back as the Old Testament or Torah, wherein it is written: "If thou lend money to any of my people that is poor by thee, thou shalt not be to him as an usurer, neither shalt thou lay upon him usury."[21]

---

[21]Exodus 22:25.

However, allowances made for compensating a lender for loss of use of the money and risk of non-repayment, as opposed to "exorbitant" interest that is equated with profiteering, have made for line-drawing issues starting seemingly as soon as the practice was generally prohibited. Modern theory tends to treat any theory of interest as part of the general theory of value and price (thus, for example, the amount of interest charged is theoretically mediated by market exchange just like the price of any other good or service), so the earlier taint associated with charging excessive interest has for the most part been eliminated.

Mercantilism

In the history of economic thought, the period from roughly 1450 through 1750 is known as the Mercantile period. Thus, Mercantilism can be understood as a bridge between feudalism and capitalism, which is tied to the rise of the defense of greater individual liberty in the eighteenth century and the Industrial Revolution in the nineteenth century. The feudalism that prevailed with the fall of the Roman Empire was characterized by economically, socially, and politically self-sufficient manors gradually giving way to increasing trade both locally and over greater distances. This led to the growth of cities outside the manor and the emergence and growth of the nation-state. Economies that had been largely local in character increasingly expanded toward a national scale. There were markets that sold various products including cloth, yarn, wine, leather, shoes, and wheat. Ships brought products from increasing distances. Banks and currency exchanges appeared, first in Italy and then in northern Europe, and became a regular feature of commercial activity. The merchant emerged from the feudal shadows to become a distinctive figure with increasing social acceptance, prestige, and power. Accompanying these developments were (1) the European "discovery" of the New World and the Far East; (2) a great inflow of gold and silver; and (3) the emergence and consolidation of power and authority in the nation-state. With the rise of the nation-state came a close association of state interest and merchant interest.[22]

---

[22]*See* Galbraith, pp. 32–37.

Economic thinking expanded from its focus on individuals, households, and producers to the analysis of the economy as a system of laws, sectors, and interrelationships of its own. Unlike earlier times, when economics was the work of philosophers, in the mercantile world economic analysis was the province of statesmen, bureaucrats, bankers, and merchants.[23] During this period, Mercantilism did not have one generally recognized spokesperson. Moreover, as we shall see, the cluster of beliefs included within Mercantilism underwent considerable evolution and revision, such that a number of the tenets advanced as gospel in the early and middle period were rejected and refuted by later authors who, although writing during that period, advanced principles that Adam Smith was able to draw upon in *The Wealth of Nations.*

Although practiced with considerable variation by virtually every European nation-state of the time, the mercantilists were united in the goal of making and maintaining a strong nation-state by strengthening its political and economic power.[24] With some variation and evolution over time, Mercantilism was widely accepted as mainstream doctrine in some form by nations throughout Europe, including England, Holland, Spain, France, Germany, Flanders, and Scandinavia.

Ekelund and Hebert point out that there are two common ways of viewing the development of theory and practice associated with Mercantilism.[25] On the one hand, one may take a static, doctrinal, or ideational view, which approaches Mercantilism as a discrete set of objectively determined rules, many of which were eventually replaced by a more classically liberal perspective. Alternatively, one may take a dynamic and process- or policy-based view, which sees Mercantilism as part of a running theme of rational self-interest operating within a given set of institutional constraints. The latter school of thought fits in well with the story of rational self-interest as a manifestation of permanent natural law, which (in the view of its proponents) is ultimately impossible to deny and is inextricably tied to progress.

---

[23] *See generally*, A. Gray. 1931. *The Development of Economic Doctrine: An Introductory Survey* (New York: Longmans), p. 74.

[24] *See* J.F. Bell, *A History of Economic Thought,* 2d ed., (Huntington, New York: Robert E. Krieger Publishing Company), pp. 55–56 (hereinafter, "Bell").

[25] Ekelund and Hebert, at p. 46.

In Mercantilism, one can also see a shift from the Scholastic focus on justice and salvation to a more secular focus on wealth and power.[26] Nevertheless, throughout most of the period, Mercantilism shared the earlier Platonic
assumption that, contrary to Adam Smith's subsequent analysis, there existed a fundamental conflict between the pursuit of private interests (private
wealth maximization) and the welfare of the society as a whole.[27] Accordingly,
there was a strong belief in (1) the need for state regulation and intervention in the economy, (2) monopolies and monopolistic control of prices, and
(3) the accumulation of gold and silver, which should be the goal of personal
and public policy and to which personal effort and public regulation should
always be directed.[28] Unlike Adam Smith and the market economists that
followed, the early mercantilists did not see win–win benefits flowing from
free trade, but rather saw trade as a zero-sum game.[29]

Viewing it in the interest of both the state and influential merchants,
Mercantilism focused on international trade and finance, especially as a
means to accumulate gold. One commonly cited exposition of mercantil-
ist principles can be found in the appropriately titled book, "*Austria Over
All, If Only She Wills It*," which was published in 1684 by Philipp von
Hörnigk. In this book, von Hörnigk set forth the following nine points:

> First: the nature of the country must be exactly observed and sur-
> veyed, every corner, every clod of earth examined to see whether it
> be cultivable. Every useful plant under the sun shall be examined
> to see whether it could flourish in the country and how well, since
> the proximity of the sun, or its reverse, is not everything. In all that
> concerns gold and silver, no labor or expense should be spared to
> bring them to light.
>
> Secondly, all commodities in a country which cannot be used raw are
> to be processed at home. . . .
>
> Thirdly, ... Regard must . . . be had to populating a country with as
> many men as it can support. . . . And all possible ways and means

---

[26]*See generally*, Galbraith, at pp. 37–38.

[27]*See generally*, Bell, p. 77.

[28]*See generally*, Galbraith, at pp. 39–41.

[29]*See generally*, Galbraith, at p. 39.

must be found to bring these men out of idleness into productive employment, [and] to teach them and encourage them. . . .

Fourthly, gold and silver, once in the country . . . are in no way or fashion, . . . to be allowed to leave it again, nor allowed to remain buried in chests and strongboxes, but always kept in circulation; nor are they to be allowed to be fashioned into forms where they are, as it were, made useless and unserviceable. . . .

Fifthly, the inhabitants are to be most strongly enjoined to content themselves with their domestic products. . . .

Sixthly, what is indispensable . . . should wherever possible not be bought directly from abroad for gold or silver, but be exchanged against other domestic products.

Seventhly, such foreign products shall then be acquired in their raw state and processed at home and the cost of manufacture earned there.

Eighthly, day and night watch must be kept that surplus home products be sold abroad in manufactured form . . . and for gold and silver, and to this end consumers must be sought out, so to speak, from the ends of the world and exports promoted in every way.

Ninthly . . . products available domestically in sufficient quantity and of adequate quality should never be allowed to be imported; no sympathy or pity for the foreigner should affect this policy . . . .

As mentioned earlier, the mercantilists generally equated the nation's store of gold with wealth (as opposed to, for example, the goods enjoyed by the people) and viewed the competition for gold among the nations as a zero-sum game. Many of them thus made favorable balance-of-trade a priority and seemed oblivious to the possibility of win–win exchange between nations. During the later mercantile period, David Hume (1711–1776) showed that attempts to maintain a lopsided trade balance were unsustainable by pointing out that as the amount of gold bullion a nation possessed and monetized as currency within an economy increased, the price of domestic goods would rise because as the supply of coins increased, the value of any one coin decreased, thereby leading to a rise in prices. This would ultimately result in less of the now more expensive exports being sold, and more of the less expensive imports being bought—resulting in a return to trade balance, all other things being equal. This concept reflects the quantity theory of money, which roughly states that the quantity of money in circulation is inversely related to the value of money.[30]

While the majority of existing property rights during this period resided in the monarch, that same monarch nevertheless depended to some meaningful extent on the merchants to fill the monarch's coffers with gold bullion, which led to the granting of legal monopolies to favored merchants in the form of franchises like the East India Company. Protection of favored merchants from outside competition also operated on a more local level, such as the city of London restricting the use of foreign technology or hiring of foreign firms through the employment of licensing regimes. The generation of profits via monopoly power and political patronage rather than competitive advantage has been referred to as "rent-seeking," and continues to be an issue today.

Another issue that aligned moneyed merchants and landed aristocracy was the "utility of poverty."[31] The general idea was that, "[e]veryone but an idiot knows that the lower classes must be kept poor or they will never be industrious."[32] Accordingly, unemployment was considered to be nothing more than a problem of indolence.[33] Furthermore, education was seen (at least by some) as wasted on the poor:

> Reading, writing, and arithmetic . . . are very pernicious to the poor . . . every hour those poor people spend at their book is so much time lost to the society. Going to school, in comparison to working, is idleness, and the longer boys continue in this easy sort

---

[30]*See generally*, Landreth and Colander, at p. 39. The quantity theory of money was recognized as early as 1569 by Frenchman Jean Bodin and further developed by John Locke (1632–1704), who demonstrated that the level of economic activity in an economy depends on the quantity of money and its velocity. More on this subject will be discussed later.

[31]E.S. Furniss. 1920. *The Position of the Laborer in a System of Nationalism* (Boston: Houghton Mifflin), p. 117.

[32]A. Young. 1771. *The Farmer's Tour Through the East of England* (London).

[33]According to contemporary free-market theory, unemployment may be deemed a voluntary preference for leisure.

of life, the more unfit they will be when grown up for downright labour . . . . Men who are to remain and end their days in a laborious, tiresome, and painful station of life, the sooner they are put upon it at first, the more patiently they will submit to it ever after.[34]

Essentially, Mercantilism supported the notion that "the nation's destiny was conditioned upon a numerous population of unskilled laborers, driven by the very competition of numbers to a life of constant industry at minimum wages."[35] In such a society, submission and contentment among the working class "could be fostered by a destruction of social ambition among its members."[36]

From the process perspective, the decline of Mercantilism can be attributed at least in part to the undermining of the power of monarchy to ensure that the benefits of monopoly power justified the costs borne by merchants in order to acquire it. This undermining of power came in part from nonparticipating merchants who were able to act competitively outside the protectionist system and in part from a parliament and judiciary that was growing more and more independent.[37] At least in part, the system's demise was arguably inevitable to the extent it truly constituted a form of rent-seeking (i.e., noncompetitive or monopoly-based profit-seeking) because rent-seeking diverts at least some meaningful amount of wealth on the basis of political power rather than productive capacity and eventually either (1) faces some form of uprising by those excluded from participation in what would otherwise reasonably be expected to be a wealth-creating system or (2) simply gives way to a more productive system. Of course, there is always some risk that those

---

[34]B. Mandeville. 2006. "Essay on Charity and Charity Schools," in *Education Documents, England And Wales 800 To 1816: VOLUME 1,* ed. D.W. Sylvester (Routledge), p. 180.

[35]E.S. Furniss. 1920. *The Position of the Laborer in a System of Nationalism; A Study in the Labor Theories of the Later English Mercantilists* (New York: Houghton Mifflin), p. 150.

[36]*Id.*

[37]The undermining of monarchial power was also aided by the ongoing development of technology.

empowered by a rent-seeking system will be able to hold off any challenges to the status quo.

In England, the uprising by those excluded from fully participating in the mercantilist system was facilitated by competition of a somewhat different sort: the long-standing competition (1) for legislative power between the monarchy and parliament that had ensued for centuries, and also (2) for judicial power between the King's courts and the common-law courts. In practice, patents and monopolies recognized by the royal courts would not necessarily be recognized by the common-law courts or the Parliament, which could reverse common-law court decisions, and the resulting uncertainty reduced the value of benefits that the monarchy could bestow.[38]

From a doctrinal perspective, the transition from Mercantilism to liberalism can be explained at least in part by Mercantilism's loss of intellectual respectability. For example, Bernard de Mandeville, who was quoted above advancing the mercantilist "utility of poverty" doctrine, famously asserted in his *Fable of the Bees* that individuals acting purely in their self-interest would nevertheless ultimately benefit society—foreshadowing the work of Adam Smith. Mandeville's argument, however, was rooted in a rejection of metaphysical rationalization and essentially claimed that if our only source of knowledge is our sensory input, and every individual is privy to a different set of inputs, then the best path forward for society would be to allow those individuals to act on the information they receive as freely as possible.[39] Mandeville also espoused a subjective view of value, which further advanced the notion that individuals should be free to pursue their self-interest, since it was impossible to agree on a common standard of the good to be enforced by regulation.[40] Finally, the role of technological advances during the seventeenth and eighteenth centuries should not be understated. Technological disruption makes it difficult to

---

[38]Ekelund and Hebert, at pp. 60–65.

[39]Recall this idea when our discussion moves to the Austrian school of economics.

[40]One might also chart a path of ideas from power to liberty by moving from Thomas Hobbes (1588–1679) and Niccolo Machiavelli (1469–1527) to David Hume (1711–1776) and John Locke (1632–1704), to name just a few.

maintain a mercantilist regulatory regime because the innovations allow competition beyond the existing scheme of control.

The Physiocrats

All of this brings us to the Physiocrats, who formed the final leg of the journey to Adam Smith and the dawn of capitalism. To the extent our discussion of Mercantilism up to this point has been focused primarily on England, we will now turn our attention to France, which imposed an even more comprehensive form of Mercantilism than England, and subsequently gave rise to a more prominent resistance movement. We will begin our discussion by examining some of the influential thinkers who paved the way for the shift from Mercantilism to physiocracy.

One of the individuals paving the way from Mercantilism to the Physiocrats was Pierre de Boisguilbert (1646–1714). Boisguilbert was a French magistrate whose frustrations with the decline of France as an economic power led him to formulate a number of critiques. First, he challenged the mercantilist notion that money equaled wealth. Rather, money was a means to an end: "Gold and silver are not and never have been wealth in themselves, and are of value only in relation to, and in so far as they can procure, the things necessary for life, for which they serve merely as a gauge and an evaluation."[41] What was important, according to Boisguilbert, was not merely how much money a nation had, but rather how effectively the money was invested in productive enterprise. In other words, a healthy economy had a lot of buying and selling (production and consumption) going on.

Boisguilbert's second criticism of France's mercantilist policies had to do with taxation, which did put money into the hands of the monarchy, but at significantly greater cost to the economy as a whole. Boisguilbert was critical both of the unfairness of a tax system that exempted many of the privileged citizens (and was otherwise applied in a capricious manner) and the role certain taxes played in stifling production, consumption, and trade. Finally, Boisguilbert criticized policies that interfered with free

---

[41]*See* C.W. Cole. 1943. *French Mercantilism 1683–1700* (New York: Columbia University Press), p. 242 (quoting Boisguilbert).

trade generally. Boisguilbert saw free trade (at least to a point) as an antidote for the ill effects mercantilist policies had manifested in his country.

Another important writer of the time, whose contributions were only truly appreciated later but who nonetheless captured the relevant zeitgeist, was Richard Cantillon (1680–1734). Cantillon's highly regarded book, "*An Essay on the Nature of Trade in General*," was described by the famous British neoclassical economist William Stanley Jevons as "the cradle of political economy" and "the first systematic Treatise on Economics," accolades more commonly ascribed to Adam Smith.[42] While Boisguilbert sought practical solutions to discrete economic problems, Cantillon was seeking to understand the underlying basic principles that animated economies just as Isaac Newton had advanced regarding the universe.

Foreshadowing Adam Smith, Cantillon described a market system wherein entrepreneurs adjust production in response to demand until a sort of equilibrium is reached, such that the price of a good is high enough to cover the costs of actual production as well as justify the opportunity cost incurred by the entrepreneur in not producing other goods, but also low enough to not drive consumers to seek alternative goods or simply do without the good (note in the following the distinction between "real and intrinsic value" and "market price"):

> If the farmers in a state sow more corn than usual, much more than is needed for the year's consumption, the real and intrinsic value of the corn will correspond to the land and labour which enter into its production; but as there is too great an abundance of it and there are more sellers than buyers the market price of the corn will necessarily fall below the intrinsic price of value. If on the contrary the farmers sow less corn than is needed for consumption there will be more buyers than sellers and the market price of corn will rise above its intrinsic value.[43]

---

[42]W.S. Jevons. 1881. "Richard Cantillon and the Nationality of Political Economy," *Contemporary Review* 39, pp. 61–80.

[43]R. Cantillon. 1730. *Essai sur la Nature du Commerce in Général (Essay on the Nature of Trade in General)* (London: Frank Cass and. Co., Ltd.).

Furthermore, Cantillon advanced our understanding of how the supply of money impacts prices:

> Everybody agrees that the abundance of money or its increase in exchange, raises the price of everything. . . . Locke lays it down as a fundamental maxim that the quantity of produce and merchandise in proportion to the quantity of money serves as the regulator of market price. . . . The great difficulty of this question consists in knowing in what way and in what proportion the increase of money raises prices.[44]

Cantillon reasoned that similar monetary changes can have different effects on prices depending on where, and through whom, money passes into the system.

Thus, we arrive at the Physiocrats, who published most of their works between 1756 and 1778, and who were led by Francois Quesnay, court physician to Louis XV, as well as an acquaintance of Adam Smith. The Physiocrats sought to address the economic woes of France by coming to understand economic growth as part of an organic, natural system ("Physiocracy" means "rule of nature"). In the economy of their time (as well as the present) more goods were produced than were needed to cover the costs of producing those goods. The search for the source of this surplus led Physiocrats to the concept of "net product." In agriculture, for example, after paying all the costs of production (which they identified as seed, labor, and machinery), there was a net product which they attributed to the productivity of nature. Physiocrats believed that labor could only produce enough to pay for the cost of labor. The same logic applied to all factors of production except land.[45] Manufacturing and other non-agricultural production was "sterile" because it created no net product. Because land was the only factor capable of creating a net product, the Physiocrats concluded that land rent was the measure of a society's net product. A modern understanding of this analysis ascribes a fundamental

---

[44] *Id.*

[45] It is noteworthy that Adam Smith had sympathy for the notion that agriculture was a more productive enterprise than other industries.

error in focusing on physical productivity instead of value productivity, which will be discussed later.[46]

Noting that the circulation of blood is essential to the health of the body, the Physiocrats argued that the circulation of money is essential to the health of the economy. Thus, they argued for tax reform that would take some of the burden of financing the monarchy off the farmers and place it on to the previously exempt landowners, in order to allow the farmers to accumulate more capital that would in turn be directed toward more production. This increased production should, the Physiocrats argued, be further encouraged by the elimination of mercantilist trade restrictions. According to the Physiocrats, once these unnatural and unhealthy burdens were lifted, the circulation of income and expenditures would be restored and France's economy could start to head back in the right direction.

The Physiocrats have been criticized on at least two fronts. First, their scheme recognized farming as the only productive occupation, without any theory of value to support distinguishing farmers from manufacturers or service providers. Second, the Physiocrats' preference for agriculture lent credence to the uniqueness of land and, thereby, the nobility that owned it. Thus, the Physiocrats have been accused of trying to mount a return to feudalism rather than the developing industrialization that led to capitalism.[47]

Meanwhile, a parallel challenge to Mercantilism was taking root in Spain, which, like France, was suffering from significant economic decline viewed by many as a direct consequence of mercantilist policies. Count Pedro Rodriguez de Campomanes was one of the intellectual leaders on this front, advancing among other things the notion that the concentration of property in the hands of the few (the monarch, the aristocracy, and the Catholic Church), along with restraints on the transfers of that property, interfered with economic growth. Campomanes argued that widespread ownership of property, together with free trade, was required to encourage productivity. While there is some dispute surrounding authorship, Campomanes is

---

[46]*See generally*, Landreth and Colander, at pp. 50–51.

[47]*See generally*, D. McNally. 1990. *Political Economy and the Rise of Capitalism: A Reinterpretation* (Berkeley, University of California Press), pp. 86–87.

believed by many to have published "*Discurso sobre el foment de la industria popular*" (*Discourse on the Promotion of Popular Industry*) in 1774, a mere two years before Adam Smith published his "*Wealth of Nations.*" Joseph Schumpeter was so impressed with the work that he suggested Campomanes had little to learn from the *Wealth of Nations*.[48]

Transition: From Mercantilism and the Physiocrats to the Classical Economists

In addition to all the foregoing, the emergence of capitalism was also arguably furthered by the religious upheaval of the Reformation. Looking back on the period, Max Weber, in his famous work, "*The Protestant Ethic and the Spirit of Capitalism*" (1904), argued that a culture praising "the earning of more and more money combined with the strict avoidance of all spontaneous enjoyment of life"[49] was instrumental in allowing capitalism to emerge. Wrote Weber of this Protestant culture: "The earning of money within the modern economic order is, so long as it is done legally, the result and the expression of virtue and proficiency in a calling."[50]

Obviously, whatever credence one gives to Weber's arguments, many other contributors to the rise of capitalism are easily recognizable, including inventions like the printing press (c. 1440) and the adoption of the scientific method. Certain levels of political stability are required to allow people to make the credible commitments required to finance capital investment and maintain confidence in the private property rights that promised an owner's return on investment. As Ekelund and Hebert point out, even the "Black Death" plague had a role to play by creating a labor shortage that prompted broader land ownership (as land conveyances were used to compete for labor) as well as greater investments in capital (as opposed to labor, which was in short supply), which in turn prompted innovation that spurred the Industrial Revolution.[51]

---

[48]J.A. Schumpeter. 1954. *History of Economic Analysis* (London: Routledge), pp. 172–73.

[49]P. 53.

[50]Pp. 53–54.

[51]Ekelund and Hebert, at p. 98.

Returning briefly to Mercantilism, we pause to note that although many, if not most, of the mercantile principles have been discredited by the modern understanding of economics, their contributions to the development of economic thought are noteworthy, including their recognition of the importance of analyzing the economy as a system, the interrelatedness of economic sectors, and the importance to economic understanding of empirical evidence and the quantification of economic phenomena. As noted earlier, many later mercantilists became aware of the analytical errors of their predecessors by recognizing that money is not a measure of wealth, that all nations could not have a positive trade balance, that no one country could maintain a positive trade balance over the long run, that trade was not necessarily a zero-sum game but rather could be mutually advantageous, and that nations and their citizens could benefit by increasing labor specialization and decreasing regulation. On this latter point, Sir William Petty observed: "We must consider in general, that as wiser Physicians tamper not excessively with their Patients, rather observing and complying with the motions of nature, then contradicting it with vehement Administrations of their own; so in Politicks and Oconomicks the same must be used. . . ."[52] Such growing recognition of the advantages of free trade helped pave the way for the work of Adam Smith.

One doctrinal principle of Mercantilism remains a vital issue of controversy today: the question of the neutrality or non-neutrality of money. As already noted, a tenet of Mercantilism was that changes in the supply of money lead to changes in the real output of the economy. In contrast, Adam Smith and the other classical economists believed that the level of economic activity depends on real factors such as the quantity and quality of labor, natural resources, capital goods, technological advances, and institutional structure. Any changes in the quantity of money, they maintained, would affect neither the long-run level of output nor growth, but only the level of prices. Although the classical view of money neutrality might come as a puzzling surprise to contemporary "Fed watchers," most contemporary economists hasten to add that the neutrality of money is

---

[52]Sir W. Petty. 1899. *The Economic Writings of Sir William Petty, together with The Observations upon Bills of Mortality, more probably by Captain John Graunt* (Cambridge: Cambridge University Press), p. 60.

deemed to be a long-run phenomenon, and the consequences of central bank monetary policy are a short-run concern. However, along with famously declaring that "[i]n the long run we are all dead,"[53] J.M. Keynes, in his *General Theory*, advanced a theory of fuller employment that rests in part on the non-neutrality of money in both the short and the long run. According to Keynes, by reason of a liquidity preference, without government action capitalist economies would be on an ongoing short-run basis, stuck in under-capacity-producing equilibrium.[54] In the "Notes on Mercantilism" section of his *General Theory*, Keynes declared sound their belief that increases in the quantity of money (a natural consequence of a positive trade balance) would increase output.[55] In apparent agreement (while nevertheless noting its inflationary effect), John Kenneth Gailbraith noted that it is reasonable to assume that the presence of more money in an economic system would impact behavior as more and more people strove to acquire it.[56]

Before 1776, a number of writers offered significant insights into the dynamics of economic systems and the flawed analyses and policies of the early Mercantilists and Physiocrats, but none were able to offer a comprehensive systemic analysis that caught the widespread attention of their contemporaries. Although several others who published before Smith were similarly credited by later economists with having provided such a systemic analysis, it was only Adam Smith who achieved relatively widespread contemporary recognition of the analytical foundation established in *The Wealth of Nations*—a recognition that earned Smith almost universal acceptance as the father of political economy and modern economics.[57]

---

[53]J.M. Keynes. 1923. *A Tract on Monetary Reform* (London: Macmillan), p. 80.

[54]J.M. Keynes. 1936. *The General Theory of Employment, Interest and Money* (New Delhi, India: Atlantic Publishers & Distributors).

[55]*See generally*, Landreth and Colander, at p. 40.

[56]*See* Galbraith, at p. 35.

[57]Landreth and Colander, at p. 57.

CHAPTER 4

Classical Economics

The period between 1776 and 1870, beginning with the publication of Adam Smith's "*The Wealth of Nations*," and spanning the contributions of Jeremy Bentham, David Ricardo, Robert Malthus, and John Stuart Mill, was so rich in terms of building the structure we now know as economics that it is referred to as the classical period. Although these thinkers are frequently lumped together as part of the classical period, they had important points of disagreement, and many of the challenges they posed to one another's theories continue to intrigue and divide scholars to this day.

Adam Smith

Ekelund and Hebert describe Smith as absent-minded, unattractive, and suffering from nervous afflictions including a speech impediment—but none of this prevented him from being sought out by students as far away as Russia who wanted to hear his lectures.[1] Smith was already highly regarded before publishing "*The Wealth of Nations*," owing to his 1759 work, "*The Theory of Moral Sentiments*," in which he argued that people could act morally, despite being a fundamentally selfish creature, because they are capable of sympathizing with other people. The apparent conflict between Smith's emphasis on sympathy in "*The Theory of Moral Sentiments*" and selfishness in "*The Wealth of Nations*" was dubbed "the Adam Smith problem" by nineteenth-century German philosophers. Yet, to view the themes of these two books as a problem, rather than a grand synergistic harmony, may be missing the forest for the trees. In historical

---

[1]Ekelund and Hebert, at p. 100.

context, these books make a powerful normative and positive case for democratic self-governance that justifies freeing people from the authority of both the Church and the Crown. By the law of human nature, self-interest is balanced by compassion and endowed with the morality of the Golden Rule. Meanwhile, by the law of economics, self-interest is guided by free-market competition (as if by an invisible hand) to increasing prosperity for individuals and society.

Because Smith focused on the relation of the individual to the state, and how that relationship could best foster economic growth—which Smith saw as the primary means of bettering the human condition— his subject matter came to be referred to as political economy. As discussed above, a great deal of Smith's political economy was rooted in a belief in natural law, which was understood to trump conflicting positive law created by legislatures. A belief in natural law aligned Smith with a *laissez-faire* approach to government inasmuch as any enacted positive law could by definition be deemed inferior to the law of nature. Smith famously characterized this superiority of natural law as an "invisible hand" both in "*The Theory of Moral Sentiments*":

> [The rich] consume little more than the poor, and in spite of their natural selfishness and rapacity. . .they divide with the poor the produce of all their improvements. They are led by an invisible hand to make nearly the same distribution of the necessaries of life, which would have been made, had the earth been divided into equal portions among all its inhabitants, and thus without intending it, without knowing it, advance the interest of the society, and afford means to the multiplication of the species.[2]

and in "*The Wealth of Nations*":

> It is not from the benevolence of the butcher, the brewer, or the baker, that we expect our dinner, but from their regard to their own interest. We address ourselves, not to their humanity but to

---

[2]Part IV, Chapter I, pp. 184–5, para. 10. The reader will likely note that whatever the validity of these empirical observations at the time, they seem highly questionable in light of modern practices.

their self-love, and never talk to them of our necessities but of their advantages. . . . Every individual . . . neither intends to promote the public interest, nor knows how much he is promoting it . . . he intends only his own security; and by directing that industry in such a manner as its produce may be of the greatest value, he intends only his own gain, and he is in this, as in many other cases, led by an invisible hand to promote an end which was no part of his intention.[3]

Just as sympathy served to restrain unbridled self-interest in "*Moral Sentiments*," so competition served a similar function in "*Wealth of Nations*," and Smith warned of the anticompetitive effects of monopolies, a hallmark of Mercantilism: "People of the same trade seldom meet together, even for merriment and diversion, but the conversation ends in a conspiracy against the public, or in some contrivance to raise prices."[4] These natural regulators of sympathy and competition, which mediated self-interest as if by way of an invisible hand, were Smith's answer to the "Hobbesian dilemma," a function of the position advanced by Thomas Hobbes that asserted man's existence would be "nasty, poor, brutish and short" and a "war of all against all," absent extensive government control.[5] Conversely, attempts to manage society by authoritarian rule, be it the

---

[3]Book I, Chapter II, pp. 26–7, para 12.

[4]*The Wealth of Nations*, Book IV Chapter VIII, p. 145, para. c27.

[5]T. Hobbes. 1651. *Of Man, Being the First Part of Leviathan*, Chapter XIII: *Of the Natural Condition of Mankind as Concerning Their Felicity and Misery*. Wrote Hobbes:

"It may seem strange to some man that has not well weighed these things that Nature should thus dissociate and render men apt to invade and destroy one another; and he may therefore, not trusting to this inference made from the passions, desire perhaps to have the same confirmed by experience. Let him therefore consider with himself, when taking a journey, he arms himself and seeks to go well accompanied; when going to sleep, he locks his doors; when even in his house, he locks his chests; and this when he knows there be laws and public officers armed to revenge all injuries shall be done him; what opinion he has of his fellow-subjects when he rides armed; of his fellow-citizens, when he locks his doors; and of his children and servants, when he locks his chests. Does he not there as much accuse mankind by his actions as I do by my words?"

Church or the Crown, were doomed to failure: "[I]n the great chess-board of human society, every single piece has a principle of motion of its own, altogether different from that which the legislature might choose to impress upon it."[6] It is worth noting, however, that two years after publishing "*The Wealth of Nations*," Smith accepted a position as a state regulator, specifically the position of Commissioner of Scottish Customs and Salt Duties, which he held till his death in 1790.

In addition to self-interest, sympathy, and competition, Smith saw private property as vital to economic growth, and he explained its existence in part as a function of mankind's evolution:

> Among nations of hunters, as there is scarce any property, or at least none that exceeds the value of two or three days' labour, so there is seldom any established magistrate or any regular administration of justice. . . . civil government is not so necessary. . . . It is in the age of shepherds, in the second period of society, that the inequality of fortune first begins to take place, and introduces among men a degree of authority and subordination which could not possibly exist before. It thereby introduces some degree of that civil government which is indispensably necessary for its own preservation . . . . Civil government, so far as it is instituted for the security of property, is in reality instituted for the defence of the rich against the poor, or of those who have some property against those who have none at all.[7]

Moving on to Smith's theory of per-capita economic growth, one can summarize some of the key components as follows: (1) people's naturally occurring self-interest prompts them to trade with each other as each party pursues greater wealth; (2) the desire for greater wealth through trade encourages specialization via the division of labor, whereby each individual produces more than needed of one thing so that the excess might be traded for something more economically produced by others; (3) the introduction of money further fosters trade, since many times a counterparty to a

---

[6] *The Theory of Moral Sentiments*, Part VI, Section II, Chapter II, pp. 233–4, para 17.
[7] *Wealth of Nations*, p. 674.

trade may not have the particular item sought (which would be required for barter) but can instead provide money in exchange, which can then be used to acquire the desired item later and/or elsewhere; and (4) the entire aforementioned system rests on an ability to assess the value of the items to be exchanged. As to this last point, Smith advanced a labor theory of value (though he also recognized the role of opportunity cost and profit):

> Every man is rich or poor according to the degree in which he can afford to enjoy the necessaries, conveniences, and amusements of human life. But after the division of labour has once thoroughly taken place, it is but a very small part of these with which a man's own labour can supply him. The far greater part of them he must derive from the labour of other people, and he must be rich or poor according to the quantity of that labour which he can command, or which he can afford to purchase. The value of any commodity, therefore, to the person who possesses it, and who means not to use or consume it himself, but to exchange it for other commodities, is equal to the quantity of labour which it enables him to purchase or command. Labour, therefore, is the real measure of the exchangeable value of all commodities.[8]

One can take this analysis a step further by imagining the following sequence of events. An entrepreneur believes he will be able to produce product P at a cost that will allow him to earn a reasonable profit compared to other alternatives in light of expected demand. Should he produce too little, consumer demand will exert upward pressure on the price, but this will either encourage him to bring more P to the market or encourage competitors to do so, or both. The price will then drop as more P enters the market. Should the market then become flooded with P such that the price must be dropped in order to sell the remaining product, the production of P will be adjusted again—this time in a downward direction. This will continue till the amount produced by one or more producers is that which can be sold at a price that encourages continued production of P without the dramatic swings that occurred beforehand. This final price is often referred

---

[8] *Wealth of Nations*, p. 30.

to as the equilibrium or natural price, and can be contrasted with the actual or market price that is a function of short-term supply and demand interactions. Whether, and under what conditions, actual prices ever reach an equilibrium is a matter of considerable controversy.

One of the reasons Adam Smith favored free markets is that he believed that people, acting freely, are generally better able than highly regulated markets or managed economies to process the relevant signals to reach this equilibrium price and maximize the production and distribution of desired products. However, he did recognize that certain "public goods"—like national defense—would need to be subsidized/nationalized because "though they may be in the highest degree advantageous to a great society [they] are, however, of such a nature that the profits could never repay the expenses to any individual or small number of individuals, and which it therefore cannot be expected that any individual or small number of individuals should erect."[9]

---

[9] *Wealth of Nations*, book V, chap. 1, part 3. Smith also favored regulating the rate of interest that could be charged on loans, lest too much money be spent chasing overly risky projects:

> If the legal rate of interest in Great Britain, for example, was fixed so high as eight or ten per cent, the greater part of the money which was to be lent would be lent to prodigals and projectors, who alone would be willing to give this high interest. Sober people, who will give for the use of money no more than a part of what they are likely to make by the use of it, would not venture into the competition. A great part of the capital of the country would thus be kept out of the hands which were most likely to make a profitable and advantageous use of it, and thrown into those which were most likely to waste and destroy it. Where the legal rate of interest, on the contrary, is fixed but a very little above the lowest market rate, sober people are universally preferred, as borrowers, to prodigals and projectors. The person who lends money gets nearly as much interest from the former as he dares to take from the latter, and his money is much safer in the hands of the one set of people than in those of the other. A great part of the capital of the country is thus thrown into the hands in which it is most likely to be employed with advantage.

Id. at p. 340. *But see*, J. Bentham. 1787. *Defence of Usury* (London, UK: Payne and Foss) (arguing that economic growth requires innovation frequently ushered in by risky ventures that would never get funded if interest rate ceilings were in place).

Much of the foregoing also led Smith to again decry monopolies, as well as government-enforced trade secrets:

> A monopoly granted either to an individual or to a trading company has the same effect as a secret in trade or manufactures. The monopolists, by keeping the market constantly understocked, by never fully supplying the effectual demand, sell their commodities much above the natural price, and raise their emoluments, whether they consist in wages or profit, greatly above their natural rate.[10]

It is worth noting that in the foregoing paragraph "effectual demand" means the demand of those who desire the product and can afford to pay the price required to cover production costs (i.e., wages, profit and rent). It can be contrasted with aggregate demand, which is simply made up of all those who desire the product. To the extent that wages, profit, and rent can also be described as prices, Ekelund's and Hebert's description of Smith's concept of natural value as tautological deserves mention.[11] Smith does, however, analyze the factors of production in more detail, though we will only briefly delve into that analysis here.

As to wages, Smith notes that while in the "original state of things" everyone labored and "the whole produce of labour belongs to the labourer," once the "appropriation of land and the accumulation of stock [i.e., capital]" emerged as institutions of private property, the laborer had to look to landowners for land to farm and to capitalists for wages and tools to maximize productivity.[12] From there, Smith essentially applies an equilibrium analysis as he did to product prices. On the effectual demand side, the "wages-fund" (the supply of capital available to pay workers) serves as the ability to pay for production, which caps the desire for particular skills to be acquired and/or tasks to be performed. On the supply side, laborers must earn at least a subsistence wage and typically require more to acquire certain skills

---

[10] *Wealth of Nations*, p. 61.

[11] *See* Ekelund and Hebert, at p. 120.

[12] *Wealth of Nations*, p. 64.

and/or perform certain tasks. Smith also recognized contractual bargaining as a factor:

> What are the common wages of labour, depends everywhere upon the contract usually made between those two parties, whose interests are by no means the same. The workmen desire to get as much, the masters to give as little as possible. The former are disposed to combine in order to raise, the latter in order to lower the wages of labour.[13]

The wages-fund doctrine cited above also makes up a key part of Smith's vision of ongoing economic growth. Capitalists are encouraged to save and invest on the basis of the future profit-generating potential of accumulated capital. This accumulated capital, among other things, serves to increase the wages-fund, which allows for the hiring of more and/or better workers. These new/better workers lead to greater productivity, which leads to greater profit, which leads to more saving and investment, and the cycle repeats itself.[14]

The system created by Adam Smith in *Wealth of Nations* was relatively quickly added to by Jeremy Bentham's utilitarianism, Robert Malthus's populationisim, and advancing monetary theory, and we turn to these additions next.

Jeremy Bentham

To begin our transition, we note that one may say that self-interest, or the doctrine of utility, is the underlying philosophy of political economy as formulated by Adam Smith. That is to say, human beings are primarily driven by a desire to acquire benefits and avoid costs, and any attempt to explain, predict, or govern human behavior without taking this desire into account

---

[13] *Wealth of Nations*, p. 66.

[14] For a more detailed chain of economic growth as proposed by Smith, see Ekelund and Hebert at p. 129 (starting with the division of labor). *Compare* Ekelund and Hebert, at p. 132 (noting that although Smith highlighted the benefits of labor specialization, he also recognized specialization's potential for labor's alienation—not unlike Karl Marx).

is doomed to fail. Jeremy Bentham (1748–1832) characterized it this way in his *Introduction to the Principles of Morals and Legislation* (1789):

> Nature has placed mankind under the governance of two sovereign masters, pain and pleasure. It is for them alone to point out what we ought to do, as well as to determine what we shall do. . . . every effort we can make to throw off our subjection, will serve but to demonstrate and confirm it. . . . The principle of utility recognizes this subjection, and assumes it for the foundation of that system, the object of which is to rear the fabric of felicity by the hands of reason and of law. Systems which attempt to question it, deal in sounds instead of sense, in caprice instead of reason, in darkness instead of light.[15]

However, while Smith arguably believed in a natural identity of interest, such that order and harmony would arise naturally where individuals are free to pursue their self-interest, Bentham believed an artificial identity of interest was required for order, and that it was the legislature's job to align the interests of individuals in such a way as to, for example, minimize the incidence of crime. This was consistent with Bentham's skepticism regarding natural law: "[T]he only rational question . . . is, whether, in point of *utility*, . . . a right *ought* to be given . . . or not? To talk of a *Law of Nature*, giving . . . a *natural right*, is so much sheer nonsense. . . ."[16] The yardstick for this type of legislation is commonly stated as "the greatest happiness for the greatest number," which requires a complicated computation that Bentham acknowledged was not practical—though he insisted on application of the general principle. Money could be used as one way to calculate utility, and individual differences in utility were to be glossed over via normative judgments regarding what was good for the community (and thus assumed to be good for the individual). Of course, using money as a proxy for utility means the needs and desires of the poor will most likely be discounted.

---

[15] *Introduction to the Principles of Morals and Legislation*, at p. 17.
[16] *Supply without Burden*, pp. 93–94.

Robert Malthus

In *An Essay on the Principle of Population*, Thomas Robert Malthus (1766–1834) responded to some of the utopian optimism of his day (resulting from the great rise in per-capita production that accompanied the Industrial Revolution) by pointing out that the combination of scarcity of resources (particularly food) and overpopulation would inevitably thwart any march to utopia—in fact, it would result in a subsistence economy.[17] While highlighting the import of population growth for economic analysis, among other shortcomings Malthus likely underestimated the ability of innovation to combat scarcity and control fertility, and failed to foresee that a stable middle class living well above subsistence might voluntarily limit children. Nonetheless, it remains true that excessive population growth can seriously dampen per capita economic growth—particularly in developing countries.

As an aside, it may be worth repeating here that even at this early stage of the development of political economy, theorists sought to define the effect money has on economic activity. One early view advanced the mercantile notion that money stimulated trade, since it was necessary to facilitate ready exchange, and thus an abundance of money equaled wealth. On the other side of this debate were those who argued that money was neutral, which is to say that changes in the amount of money would not impact wealth because prices would rise and fall in relation to the quantity of money available. While the former theory was rejected after the inflationary effects of increasing a nation's money supply were realized, the latter view was qualified to account for the fact that money was not perfectly neutral because changes in the money supply were shown to impact employment, output, and productivity. Additional debates surrounding money involved questions of "hard money" versus paper currencies, and whether any paper currency should be either expressly limited in quantity or tied to a particular form of "hard money" like gold. Many of these debates continue to the current day.[18]

---

[17]The full title of the essay is, *An Essay on the Principle of Population as It Affects the Future Improvement of Society, with Remarks on the Speculations of Mr. Godwin, M. Condorcet, and Other Writers.*

[18]*Cf.* The Economist. December, 2011. *Marginal Revolutionaries*, available at http://www.economist.com/node/21542174?mid=5655 (identifying Modern Monetary

David Ricardo

David Ricardo (1772–1823), in his *Principles of Political Economy and Taxation*, continued the analysis of how changes occur in the distribution of income among labor, land, and other real capital, as well as how these changes impact savings and growth. Ricardo advanced the notion of a stationary equilibrium state, which added to Malthus's predictions regarding wages ultimately resting at subsistence levels due to the pressure of incessant population growth by noting that profits also would be squeezed—particularly by the increasing rent payments required to expand production growth[19]—to a point just slightly above zero. However, Ricardo, like Malthus, also arguably failed to account for innovation.

While Ricardo and Malthus essentially agreed on the foregoing theoretical propositions, they disagreed on almost everything else, including the benefits of free trade, the proper theory of value, the validity of "Say's Law" (which posited that supply creates its own demand),[20] and the proper method for economic analysis. As to this last point, Ricardo wrote to Malthus in one of their many correspondences:

Theory as arguing that the use of modern paper currency frees government from prior financial constraints because the currency is created by the state); L.R. Wray. June, 2011. "Modern Money Theory: A Primer on Macroeconomics for Sovereign Monetary Systems," *New Economic Perspectives*, available at http://neweconomicperspectives.org/2011/06/modern-money-theory-primer-on.html.

[19]Ekelund and Hebert provide some calculations underlying this conclusion. *See* Ekelund and Hebert, p. 163.

[20]Jean-Baptiste Say (1767–1832) wrote:

> It is worthwhile to remark that a product is no sooner created than it, from that instant, affords a market for other products to the full extent of its own value. When the producer has put the finishing hand to his product, he is most anxious to sell it immediately, lest its value should diminish in his hands. Nor is he less anxious to dispose of the money he may get for it; for the value of money is also perishable. But the only way of getting rid of money is in the purchase of some product or other. Thus the mere circumstance of creation of one product immediately opens a vent for other products.

A Treatise on Political Economy, p. 138. *See also generally*, T. Sowell. 2015. *Say's Law: An Historical Analysis* (Princeton: Princeton University Press).

I am always glad to hear that you are preparing for the press; for, though I do not always agree in opinion with you, I am sure that your writings will contribute towards the progress of a science in which I take great interest. I should be more pleased that we did not so materially differ. If I am too theoretical (which I really believe is the case), you I think are too practical. There are so many combinations and so many operating causes in Political Economy that there is great danger in appealing to experience in favour of a particular doctrine, unless we are sure that all the causes of variation are seen and their effects duly estimated.[21]

In most, if not all, of these debates, Ricardo seemed to win the day, at least in part due to the fact that he admitted no doubt about his conclusions while Malthus was more cautious.[22] Furthermore, Ricardo also provided a methodological consistency and a means to clear policy proposals, which was very attractive to the fledgling economists of the time. However, in the long run very little of Ricardo's analysis stuck in the mainstream, although his theory of comparative advantage is taught to this day. He offered this theory to explain how countries are better off if they engage in trade even with nations that are less productive (the benefit flows from differential opportunity costs and is sometimes simply explained by imagining a father at a campsite who is better at every necessary activity than his son but will still benefit from assigning certain tasks to the son). Although still taught in many contexts as absolute truth, there are many sound economic reasons to doubt its applicability in real-world contexts.[23]

---

[21]J. Bonar. 1887. *Letters of David Ricardo to Thomas Robert Malthus 1810–1823* (Oxford, UK: Clarendon).

[22]Ekelund and Hebert include Nassau Senior in their discussion of Malthus and Ricardo. *See* Ekelund and Hebert, at p. 169. Due to space constraints, we omit discussion of Senior's contributions—but encourage the interested reader to follow-up with relevant research. *See also* Marian Bowley, *Nassau Senior and Classical Economics* (Routledge).

[23]*See generally*, R. Prasch. 1996. "Reassessing Comparative Advantage," *Review of Political Economy* 8, pp. 37.

John Stuart Mill

John Stuart Mill (1806–1873) is perhaps best known for his works *On Liberty* (1859) and *Utilitarianism* (1863), but it is his *Principles of Political Economy* (1848) that primarily concerns us here. Ekelund and Hebert describe the book as a bridge between the old school of economics, which they align with the years 1776 to 1870, and the new, which they align with the years 1871 to 1920, marking the rise of neoclassical economics as the prevailing orthodoxy.[24] In the preface of *Principles of Political Economy*, Mill explains:

> For practical purposes, Political Economy is inseparably inter-twined with many other branches of Social Philosophy. Except on matters of mere detail, there are perhaps no practical questions, even among those which approach nearest to the character of purely economical questions, which admit of being decided on economical premises alone. And it is because Adam Smith never loses sight of this truth; because, in his applications of Political Economy, he perpetually appeals to other and often far larger considerations than pure Political Economy affords—that he gives that well-grounded feeling of command over the principles of the subject for purposes of practice.... It appears to the present writer that a work similar in its object and general conception to that of Adam Smith, but adapted to the more extended knowledge and improved ideas of the present age, is the kind of contribution which Political Economy at present requires.[25]

This expressed humility regarding the place of economics among other social sciences, and as regards its application to solving practical problems, helps explain Mill's distinction between laws of production, which may be fixed and subject to pure economic analysis, and laws of distribution, which are ultimately malleable and subject to a variety

---

[24]Ekelund and Hebert, at p. 202.

[25]*Principles*, pp. xxvii–xxviii.

of perspectives. One can see an example of this in his treatment of the stationary state, which most classical economists agreed was ultimately inevitable but to be avoided to whatever extent possible. Mill thought arrival of the stationary state could be a good thing because questions of distribution and justice could then be addressed more directly:

> I cannot, therefore, regard the stationary state of capital and wealth with the unaffected aversion so generally manifested towards it by political economists of the old school. I am inclined to believe that it would be, on the whole, a very considerable improvement on our present condition. I confess I am not charmed with the ideal of life held out by those who think that the normal state of human beings is that of struggling to get on; that the trampling, crushing, elbowing, and treading on each other's heels, which form the existing type of social life, are the most desirable lot of human kind, or anything but the disagreeable symptoms of one of the phases of industrial progress.[26]

Mill also was very willing to accept government interference in a capitalist economy wherever it might serve some greater good than deferring to strict *laissez-faire* policies. He noted a number of areas, like consumer protection, preservation of the environment, and public utility regulation, which allowed for government intervention. For example, he believed in "death duties," which limited the ability of individuals to inherit wealth that was not tied to any productivity of their own:

> Were I framing a code of laws according to what seems to me best in itself, without regard to existing opinions and sentiments, I should prefer to restrict, not what any one might bequeath, but what any one should be permitted to acquire, by bequest or inheritance. Each person should have power to dispose by will of his or her whole property; but not to lavish it in enriching some one individual, beyond a certain maximum, which should be fixed sufficiently high to afford the means of comfortable independence.

---

[26]*Principles*, p. 748.

The inequalities of property which arise from unequal industry, frugality, perseverance, talents, and to a certain extent even opportunities, are inseparable from the principle of private property, and if we accept the principle, we must bear with these consequences of it: but I see nothing objectionable in fixing a limit to what any one may acquire by the mere favour of others, without any exercise of his faculties, and in requiring that if he desires any further accession of fortune, he shall work for it.[27]

It is worth mentioning that Mill was greatly influenced by Auguste Comte (1798–1857), author of *The Course in Positivist Philosophy* and advocate of the Law of Three Stages, which argues that people evolve from a theological stage (belief in God) to a metaphysical stage (belief in, for example, natural law) and finally enter the positive stage (belief in science and empiricism). Although Mill did not abandon the deductive aspects of a belief in natural law so central to Adam Smith, he did aspire to increase the extent to which inductive empiricism was relied upon in economics.

Large business enterprises, particularly corporations, are a staple of modern society. Mill added to the explanation for why they exist by noting that, while Adam Smith's division of labor is "one of the principal causes of large manufactories" (because "[t]he larger the enterprise, the farther the division of labour may be carried"), so are economies of scale (because "[e]xpensive machinery . . . is not resorted to except with the intention of producing . . . as much of the article as comes up to the full powers of the machine").[28]

In 1869, Mill recanted the wages-fund doctrine in a review of a book by W. T. Thornton. Ekelund and Hebert describe this event as shaking the foundations of classical economics.[29] To review, the wages-fund doctrine posited that there is a fixed amount of capital available to pay labor during any particular production cycle. Many advocates of the doctrine took this to mean that efforts by organized labor to raise wages were futile, if not counterproductive. Mill challenged this notion of a fixed pool by arguing

---

[27] *Principles*, pp. 227–28.
[28] *Principles*, pp. 132, 135.
[29] Ekelund and Hebert, p. 198.

that capitalists could expand the pool of capital available for wages by reducing the amount they spent on themselves for nonessential goods. While Mill's argument is generally understood to have been rebutted, at least under a certain set of classical assumptions,[30] Mill's recantation of the wages-fund doctrine can be seen as part of a broader set of causes leading to the decline of classical economics. Other causes include the rise of marginalism (about which more will be said shortly) and the inroads made by critics of classical economics in light of the perceived problems created by the Industrial Revolution.

---

[30] *See* Ekelund and Hebert, p. 200.

CHAPTER 5

Socialist Economics and Other Critiques of the Classical Economists

The Industrial Revolution was obviously a boon to both England and the world in many ways. However, it also brought with it urban decay and overcrowding, abusive labor conditions, and heightened awareness of income disparities between the rich and the poor. Charles Dickens was a renowned critic of the period and had this to say about certain workhouse conditions:

> The members of this board were very sage, deep, philosophical men; and when they came to turn their attention to the work-house, they found out at once, what ordinary folks would never have discovered—the poor people liked it! It was a regular place of public entertainment for the poorer classes; a tavern where there was nothing to pay; a public breakfast, dinner, tea, and supper all the year round; a brick and mortar elysium, where it was all play and no work. "Oho!" said the board, looking very knowing; "we are the fellows to set this to rights; we'll stop it all, in no time." So, they established the rule, that all poor people should have the alternative (for they would compel nobody, not they), of being starved by a gradual process in the house, or by a quick one out of it. With this view, they contracted with the water-works to lay on an unlimited supply of water; and with a corn-factor to supply periodically small quantities of oatmeal; and issued three meals of thin gruel a day, with an onion twice a week, and half a roll on

Sundays. They made a great many other wise and humane regulations, having reference to the ladies, which it is not necessary to repeat; kindly undertook to divorce poor married people, in consequence of the great expense of a suit in Doctors' Commons; and, instead of compelling a man to support his family, as they had theretofore done, took his family away from him, and made him a bachelor! There is no saying how many applicants for relief, under these last two heads, might have started up in all classes of society, if it had not been coupled with the workhouse; but the board were long-headed men, and had provided for this difficulty. The relief was inseparable from the workhouse and the gruel; and that frightened people.[1]

The criticisms and calls for reform were a direct challenge to classical economics because it was associated with the Industrial Revolution as a cause and because it advanced theories that posited reform as futile (e.g., Say's law posited allowing self-correcting markets to restore economic health over time, and laborers could expect nothing more than subsistence wages long term).

John Stuart Mill urged charity for the poor ("human beings should help one another; and the more so, in proportion to the urgency of the need"),[2] but he also feared incentivizing indolence:

The condition of a pauper must cease to be, as it has been made, an object of desire and envy to the independent labourer. Relief must be given; no one must be allowed to starve; the necessaries of life and health must be tendered to all who apply for them; but to all who are capable of work they must be tendered on such terms, as shall make the necessity of accepting them be regarded as a misfortune; and shall induce the labourer to apply for them only when he cannot help it, and to take the first opportunity of again shifting for himself. To this end, relief must be given only in exchange for labour, and labour at least as irksome and severe

---

[1] C. Dickens. 1838. *Oliver Twist*, Ch. 2, (London, UK: Bentley's Miscellany).
[2] *Principles*, p. 960.

as that of the least fortunate among the independent labourers: relief, moreover, must be confined to necessaries.[3]

It is difficult to talk about correcting perceived injustices manifest in poverty without talking about taxation and wealth distribution. Mill was concerned with providing equal opportunity to individuals while not undermining incentives to produce. Thus, he distinguished income distribution from wealth distribution and, as earlier, argued for aggressive inheritance taxes while keeping income taxes essentially flat and low. In addition, he distinguished indirect taxes that more heavily burdened the poor (like taxes on sugar, coffee, and tea) from sumptuary taxes that targeted "snob" goods—seeking to lower the former while raising the latter. Thus, Mill was not averse to using taxation to effectuate redistribution so long as the goal was equality of opportunity, as opposed to equality of result, and incentives to work were maintained.

An issue related to poverty that was highlighted by the technological advances that spurred the Industrial Revolution was the impact of such technological disruption on employment. In the third edition of *The Principles of Political Economy and Taxation*, Ricardo posited that mechanization might undermine the labor class. This began what became known as the "Compensation Controversy," with many of the primary classical theorists like Malthus and Mill arguing that long-term unemployment due to technological innovation was unlikely because market forces would eventually lead back to an efficient equilibrium point for employment. Of course, concerns about the technological displacement of workers continue to animate economic discussions to this very day.

Sir Edwin Chadwick

Sir Edwin Chadwick (1800–1890) was a contemporary and friend of John Stuart Mill and Jeremy Bentham who, together with Nassau Senior, drafted the famous 1834 report recommending reforms of the Poor Laws of the time. He was also very active in trying to improve local sanitation

---

[3] *Proposed Reform*, p. 361.

during his day, which in some cases literally consisted of raw sewage flowing in the streets. In addition to agreeing with Mill that technology would not displace workers in the long run (something which he inferred from witnessing a street-sweeping machine displaced local street sweepers and the displaced workers migrated to other types of work), he argued that recessions were normal parts of business cycles that would drive innovation and ultimately lead to better conditions for labor. He also believed education was essential to fighting poverty, particularly if workers were going to keep up with technological advances like the use of steam power: "Unfortunately, in the present state of education in the agricultural districts, if higher wages were offered, the men were not to be found to do the work with the greatest amount of economy, and in order to attain this end, their education must be improved."[4]

Chadwick agreed with Bentham that an artificial identity of interest had to be created by arranging legal obligations and punishments in order to direct self-interested incentives in a way that would minimize public harm (recall that this differed from Adam Smith, who argued there was a natural identity of interest between private and public, such that individual self-interest would naturally be guided by competition or an invisible hand to facilitate public good). However, Chadwick simplified the complicated utility calculus of Bentham, which involved the summation of individual interests (including interpersonal utility comparisons) in order to determine the public interest, by equating the public interest with economic efficiency. That is to say, if an ordinance reduced economic waste it was deemed to be in the public interest.[5]

Chadwick further argued that both government and capitalists would benefit by investing in improving the conditions of the poor. By

---

[4] *Forces*, p. 63.

[5] To the extent utilitarianism poses a challenge to *laissez-faire* policies (i.e., rather than letting the market decide who gets what, we will study costs and benefits and allocate resources on that basis), economists favoring *laissez-faire* policies could be seen as hijacking utilitarian concepts by simply defining the results of free exchange as utility. In other words, while utilitarianism may be viewed as starting out as a challenge to *laissez-faire* ideology, once utility is equated with efficiency, and efficiency is generally associated with free-market transactions, then utilitarianism arguably becomes an asset to those espousing a *laissez-faire* ideology as opposed to a challenge.

providing more sanitary environments, including easy access to clean water, the state could reduce the spread of disease and the costs of deadly outbreaks of contagious illness, which were imposed on the entire community. By providing safe and convenient housing, as well as improved working conditions, capitalists would reap the rewards of more loyal and energetic workers who missed fewer days of work. Certainly, some in government and business would be motivated to make these changes out of benevolence, but Chadwick—like Mill and Bentham—understood the importance of incentives and believed that sometimes government action was needed to establish profit-motive in changing behavior. In addition, Chadwick argued that the government expenditures to improve sanitation (preferably via a private franchise-bidding process) were profitable to the government because fewer people would end up widowed and orphaned wards of the state, and profitable to private enterprise because laborers would be more fit for work.

In advancing these positions, Chadwick distanced himself from Mill by urging a centralization of property rights with private competition occurring via bidding for exclusive rights to provide the relevant public good. While this responded to concerns about some services never being adequately provided to maximize overall utility without government support, it also addressed concerns about the ineffectiveness of government management. Chadwick's scheme showed that it was possible to bring many of the salutary effects of competition (e.g., avoiding monopoly profits) while still centralizing the provision of public goods. Ekelund and Hebert present an example of Chadwick's plan in action when they describe a consolidation of French gas companies resulting in improved supply, decreased cost, and increased shareholder wealth.[6] Chadwick argued that these types of results proved that under certain conditions of natural monopoly, traditional competition increased consumer prices, provided inadequate services, and subjected shareholders to extra risk.

Christopher Hamlin has argued that rather than oppose *laissez-faire* capitalism, Chadwick's public health successes allowed private enterprise

---

[6]Ekelund and Hebert, p. 251.

to thrive by staving off more radical criticism of the social costs.[7] However, to whatever extent Chadwick can be characterized as a critic of capitalism, there was no shortage of other prominent figures ready to challenge the capitalist undercurrent of the Industrial Revolution. Discomfort with the unequal manner in which the wealth created by the Industrial Revolution was being distributed, as well as the squalid conditions the lower class men, women, and children labored in, led to the rise of socialism. There were also concerns expressed regarding the psychological toll of the materialism and consumerism that capitalism was perceived to foster. Wrote Henry David Thoreau:

> [M]en labor under a mistake. The better part of the man is soon plowed into the soil for compost. By a seeming fate, commonly called necessity, they are employed, as it says in an old book, laying up treasures which moth and rust will corrupt and thieves break through and steal. It is a fool's life, as they will find when they get to the end of it, if not before.[8]

The Reformers

One thing many of the anticapitalists shared with the "Father of Capitalism," Adam Smith, was a belief in progressive stages of societal development. Where they differed was as to whether capitalism was to be understood as the height of our economic evolution, or rather a somewhat bleak stepping stone to a better age. For example, the French philosopher Marquis de Condorcet (1743–1794) advanced both the notion that human evolution was subject to natural laws that could be discovered through observation, and that his observations led him to the conclusion that the critical shift leading to the next stage of human progress would be one away from a focus on the well-being of certain individuals (often at the expense of society as a whole) to one focused on the collective

---

[7]C. Hamlin. 1998. *Public Health and Social Justice in the Age of Chadwick, Britain: 1800-1854* (Cambridge, UK: Cambridge University Press).
[8]H.D. Thoreau. 1854. *Walden; or, Life in the Woods.* (Boston, MA: Ticknor and Fields).

well-being of society. This apparent tension between individual liberty and collective well-being continues to surface routinely in many modern economic debates.

As already touched upon, another aspect of humanity's progress lies in the area of technology. J. C. L. Simonde de Sismondi (1773–1842) was a Swiss economist who argued that while technological advances would bestow many benefits, they would also put pressures on workers leading to problems with unemployment and overproduction:

> Every invention in the arts, which has multiplied the power of man's work, from that of the plough to the steam engine, is useful. . . . Society had made progress only through such discoveries; it is through them that the work of man has sufficed for his needs. . . . It is not the fault of the progress of mechanical science, but the fault of the social order, if the worker, who acquires the power to make in two hours what would take him twelve to make before, does not find himself richer, and consequently does not enjoy more leisure, but on the contrary is doing six times more work than is demanded.[9]

Friedrich List (1789–1846) was a leader of the General Association of German Manufacturers and Merchants who argued that the historically progressive nature of economic development meant that one should be skeptical of proposed universal rules of economic growth. This was so because conditions that may spur growth at one point in a nation's development might actually stunt growth if applied incorrectly to some other period. Specifically, he challenged the pure free-trade focus of classical economics, albeit begrudgingly, as follows:

> [I]n nations . . . which possess all the necessary mental and material conditions and means for establishing a manufacturing power of their own, and of thereby attaining the highest degree of civilisation, and development of material prosperity and political power,

---

[9] *Nouveaux principes d'economie politique*, I, p. 349.

but which are retarded in their progress by the competition of a foreign manufacturing power which is already farther advanced than their own—only in such nations are commercial restrictions justifiable for the purpose of establishing and protecting their own manufacturing power; and even in them it is justifiable only until that manufacturing power is strong enough no longer to have any reason to fear foreign competition, and thenceforth only so far as may be necessary for protecting the inland manufacturing power in its very roots.[10]

While the preceding critics of capitalism sought to justify their reforms on the basis of laws of progress manifesting in history, the utopian socialists felt unencumbered by any such laws and argued humans and society could essentially be perfected through proper manipulation of the social environment. Robert Owen (1771–1858) challenged much of the conventional thinking when he argued in *A New View of Society* (1813) that poverty and wretchedness were not simply inherent characteristics of the working class, but rather consequences of the environment that the working poor found themselves in, and if that environment were improved so, too, would be the conduct and satisfaction of the individuals in it. He shocked many by not only suggesting such things, but actually successfully putting them into practice at his textile mill in New Lanark, Scotland. He limited child labor and improved the education, housing, wages, and overall working conditions of his laborers, while still earning substantial profits. As might have been expected, challenging the status quo in this way garnered Owen quite a bit of resentment and he was eventually forced out of his business by his partners. This experience convinced him government regulation would be required to make the changes necessary to alleviate the suffering of the working poor.

Pierre Joseph Proudhon (1809–1865) has been described by Ekelund and Hebert as a "scholastic anarchist" because he wanted to replace government with "industrial organization" and, while not completely eradicating property, sought to mandate an equal distribution thereof to avoid

---

[10] *National System*, p. 144.

power imbalances that would allow a few to earn much while working little, while most worked much and earned little.[11] He was a particular critic of classical liberalism's faith in the price mechanism as a viable means to achieving the best available ends for society, because he denied the underlying assumption that economic power was sufficiently dispersed. He went so far as to say that the law of supply and demand was a deceitful law that only assured the victory of those who own property over the rest of society.[12]

Historicism

"Historicism" describes a school of thought that questions the extent to which economic method should ignore the political, historical, and social environment. There is a German and a British school, and the German school (which can be roughly traced to 1840) can be further divided into an older and younger school, with the younger school being considered more dogmatic. Wilhelm Roscher (1817–1894) is considered the founder of the older school and is best known for his treatise *Principles of Political Economy* (1854). In this treatise he described why Ricardian economics tempted many to stay stuck on mathematical and other abstractions:

> That which is general in Political Economy has, it must be acknowledged, much that is analogous to the mathematical sciences. Like the latter, it swarms with abstractions. . . . It also, always supposes the parties to the contract to be guided only by a sense of their own best interest, and not to be influenced by secondary considerations. It is not, therefore, to be wondered at, that many authors have endeavored to clothe the laws of Political Economy in algebraic formulae. [But]. . . the advantages of the mathematical model of expression diminish as the facts to which it is applied become more complicated. This is true even in the ordinary psychology of the individual. How much more,

---

[11] *See* Ekelund and Hebert, pp. 270–71.

[12] *See* A. Ritter. 1969. *The Political Thought of Pierre-Joseph Proudhon* (Princeton, NJ: Princeton University Press), p. 121.

therefore, in the portraying of national life! . . . The abstraction according to which all men are by nature the same, different only in consequence, is one which, as Ricardo and von Thunen have shown, must pass as an indispensable stage in the preparatory labors of political economists. It would be especially well, when an economic fact is produced by the cooperation of many different factors, for the investigator to mentally isolate the factor of which, for the time being, he wishes to examine the peculiar nature. All other factors should, for a time, be considered as not operating, and as unchangeable, and then the questions asked, "What would be the effect of a change in the factor to be examined, whether the change be occasioned by enlarging or diminishing it?" But it never should be lost sight of, that such a one is only an abstraction after all, for which, not only in the transition to practice, but even in finished theory, we must turn to the infinite variety of real life.[13]

The historicists' challenge to classical economics came to a head when Gustav Schmoller (1838–1917) led the charge for the younger school headlong into Carl Menger (1840–1921), founder of the Austrian school of economics, in what came to be known as the "methodenstreit" (battle of methods). Joseph Schumpeter (1883–1950) ultimately described the controversy as likely wholly pointless because no one really ultimately disputed the importance of either historical research or analytic tools.[14] Since this section is focused on critics of capitalism, it is likely worth noting that among the many pronouncements of Schmoller was included his concern that while productivity and living standards would likely rise as a result of entrepreneurial activity, he feared the ruthlessness of the entrepreneurs themselves would lead to a rise of antisocial attitudes like greed. Meanwhile, we can note that the one thing arguably lacking from all these critics of capitalism was an analytic theory capable of standing toe-to-toe with classical economics. Karl Marx, to whom we shall turn next, attempted to provide such a theory.

---

[13] *Principles*, pp. 104–5.

[14] J.A. Schumpeter. 2006. *History of Economic Analysis* (London, UK: Routledge), p. 814.

Karl Marx

Most of the reformers of the time were seeking various forms of voluntary change, but Karl Marx considered these approaches utopian and announced:

> A spectre is haunting Europe—the spectre of Communism. . . .
> The history of all hitherto existing society is the history of class
> struggles. . . . Let the ruling classes tremble at a Communist rev-
> olution. The proletarians have nothing to lose but their chains.
> They have a world to win. Working Men of All Countries, Unite![15]

For Karl Marx, a society's method of production is not merely a means to an end utilized by individuals like some simple tool. Rather, the means of production is inextricably tied to the very nature of individuals in society because production is central to the very existence of the individual—providing the things needed for survival and well-being. Marx agreed with Adam Smith that specialization and the division of labor were key drivers to increased productivity, but he disagreed with Smith by concluding that this division of labor would ultimately lead to greater and greater conflict between individuals, whereas Smith posited harmony would result from allowing market forces to drive the division of labor in accord with natural law.

Marx was a critic of private property because he believed it allowed for the accumulation of wealth in the hands of a few at the expense of the many. He pointed out the inherent contradiction in political economy whereby the laborer is "alienated" from what he or she produces. The move can be viewed as one from Locke's argument that private property arises when individuals mix their labor with the land, to a place where property rights are used as a justification for leaving laborers with only a small part of the wealth they produce. Eventually, the masses end up essentially property-less, laboring for subsistence wages while capital continues to be further concentrated in the hands of monopolists. The social

---

[15]K. Marx and F. Engels. 1848. *Manifesto of the Communist Party* (Moscow, Russia: Progress Publishers).

institutions that thrive in this capitalist system do so because they are effective in getting the masses to conform. However, the conflict inherent in this system will eventually result in its overthrow.

A key component of Marx's theory is the concept of surplus value. Assuming that the labor required to produce a commodity establishes its value, and assuming further that capitalism can only exist if labor produces more than is required to sustain it, then the price of a good above the cost of the labor required to produce it represents surplus value that is expropriated by capitalists, thereby establishing the exploitation of labor that Marx saw as a hallmark of capitalism.

Furthermore, Marx made a number of predictions regarding capitalism, all of which would lead ultimately to revolution. First, industry would become more and more concentrated as more efficient firms drive out less efficient firms and acquire their assets. Second, a growing army of unemployed would be created by technological advances that render more and more workers superfluous. Third, since idle machinery is costly, worker misery would increase as capitalists demanded longer work days and allowed for less leisure time. Finally, economic crises and depressions would occur more frequently and create more upheaval because insatiable demand for more and more goods and profit would lead to more regular boom–bust cycles. However, in his writing Marx did not anticipate the emergence of a compromise that preserved lawful private capital acquisition within a socialist (but not communist) welfare state characterized by substantial regulation, taxation, and redistribution of private capitalist enterprise and income (rather than state ownership) as a means to provide income for the masses who own little or no capital.

CHAPTER 6

Neoclassical/Austrian Economics

Neoclassical economics, with its microeconomic focus on the firm and/ or individual as opposed to the classical macroeconomic focus on the economy as a whole,[1] as well as its rejection of purely objective formulations of value (allowing for the inclusion of subjectivity), together with its comfort with both the growing use of mathematical modeling and criticism of overdependence on these models, rose out of what was left of classical economics after it had been battered by Mill's rejection of the wages–fund doctrine, various social and socialist critiques, and Marx's broadsides against the exploitation and alienation created by the capitalism that rested on classical economics, and the inability of classical economics to respond to the pressing issues of the day, many of which revolved around the rise of railroads as discrete economic actors. Various commentators have argued that the essence of neoclassical economics resides in marginalism, the subjective theory of utility, the static analysis of resource allocation efficiency, and the promise of an equilibrium of optimal prosperity resulting from full employment of available resources.

Ekelund and Hebert describe the conventional account of the development of neoclassical economics as being launched by William Stanley Jevons in England in 1871, Carl Menger in Austria in 1871, and Leon Walras in France in 1874; Alfred Marshall is then said to have advanced

---

[1]For example, rather than focus on income, output, profits and wages, as well as population growth, on the national level as distributed among land owners, capitalists, and labor generally, a microeconomic analysis would focus on price, quantities supplied and demanded, and profits as they relate to a particular commodity or service.

the basic principles into the modern age via his *Principles of Economics* in 1890.[2] However, Ekelund and Hebert also note that this account is arguably oversimplified, and that thinkers like Antoine A. Cournot (1801–1877), Jules Dupuit (1804–1866), Hermann Heinrich Gossen (1810–1858), and J. H. von Thunen (1783–1850) provided pieces for the neoclassical puzzle before 1870.[3] What follows is a further examination of some of the key thinkers that laid the foundation for neoclassical thought.

Antoine A. Cournot

Cournot can be seen as one of the founders of the marginal revolution, around which much of microeconomic theory revolves. Cournot's analysis was offered to show that a monopolist, rather than charge the highest price possible (which, according to the law of demand would minimize the amount sold), would charge the price that will maximize profit, and this price can be found by identifying the quantity produced after which any additional item sold will add no further revenue in light of costs (i.e., the marginal profit would equal the marginal cost—or, put another way, the next unit sold "at the margin" will produce no profit in light of its cost).[4] The reason there is a limit to the quantity that can profitably be sold is because, among other things, the value of an item typically changes with the quantity available, with the market becoming essentially saturated at some point (just think for a minute how differently you would value a glass of water if you had not had anything to drink in 24 hours as opposed to having just finished your 5th glass this hour). This theory of value was in stark contrast to those of the classical school, which posited theories based on static concepts like the cost of labor. Cournot also analyzed what profit-maximizing behavior would look like in the context of a duopoly, and showed that while prices would be lower than in the case of a monopoly, they would still be higher (and fewer items would be produced) than in the case of full competition. Based on the foregoing, Cournot has

---

[2]Ekelund and Hebert, p. 454.

[3]*See* Ekelund and Hebert, pp. 456–59.

[4]*See* Ekelund and Hebert, pp. 313 (providing graphs).

been given credit for practically inventing the neoclassical theory of the firm. Cournot is also recognized as laying the foundation for the development of game theory, which was formally popularized in *The Theory of Games and Economic Behavior* published by John von Neumann and Oskar Morgenstern in 1944.[5] Finally, Cournot is often regarded as one of the primary drivers behind the role of statistical analysis in economics.

Jules Dupuit

Like Cournot, who was a mathematician, Dupuit had a significant influence on economics despite being an engineer by training. Dupuit advanced respect for economics as a science, though admittedly one more complicated than some others.

> There are weeks when the curious flock en masse to the seaside to see the greatest tides of the century. Science, which has discovered the causes of tides, tells us that on a certain day the sun and the moon will be aligned in such a way as to raise the water far above its normal level, but then it turns out that the tide does not rise as expected. Does this mean that the theory has been weakened, even in the slightest way? Can it be that the influence of the sun and the moon on the tides is suspended for a day? Of course not; this great disappointment arises because the height of the tides depends on certain causes that are amenable to calculation and on others that continue to elude science. The day on which the great tide was expected, the wind may have come from the land, so that the cause which could not be foreseen thwarted that which was predicted. And so it is with economics.[6]

---

[5]Game theory, which addresses the complexities of strategic decision making in the face of uncertain responses by other players, continues to provide fertile ground for study—in part because its conclusions can include multiple equilibria and indeterminate or suboptimal results. Interested reader may want to review W. Poundstone. 1992. *Prisoner's Dilemma: John von Neumann, Game Theory, and the Puzzle of the Bomb* (New York, NY: Doubleday).

[6]*La Liberte commercial* (In Defense of Free Trade), p. 23 (Guillaumin 1861).

Another example of his defense of economics as a science can be seen in his following explanation for short-run variance from long-run economic predictions:

> Economics might predict that free trade would lower the price of iron in France to 170 francs within a few years; but if the price falls to 120 francs instead, due to improvements in metallurgical processes, or the discovery of more abundant new minerals; or on the contrary, if the price rises to 300 francs because of the influx of gold and silver from California or Australia, these events do not refute basic principles. Of course, doubting Thomases, swayed by mere appearances and overcome by their great disdain [for abstract theory], can marshal facts in opposition to the theory, but surely intelligent people will not be convinced by their attacks.[7]

Among other things, Dupuit established "welfare economics," which is a branch of economics that proposes to measure overall social utility. Because an entire stock of merchandise can only be sold at a price that reflects the marginal utility of the last unit sold, and sellers will seek to maximize overall profit rather than unit price, some consumers will frequently obtain goods at some price lower than the maximum they would be willing to pay.[8] The difference between the price charged and the price some consumers would be willing to pay is understood to reflect social utility and is referred to as "consumer surplus." Dupuit demonstrated that even monopolies should create consumer welfare as they seek to maximize profits, and that government monopolies could create even greater consumer surplus in the provision of public goods because their goal would be to maximize consumer welfare rather than maximize profits.

Dupuit also demonstrated how price discrimination could create additional consumer welfare, and he was little concerned about criticisms of sellers who sold essentially identical items at different prices. This was so because of the subjective nature of value and the fact that he assumed

---

[7] *Id.*

[8] *See* Ekelund and Hebert, pp. 321 (providing graph).

consumers' overall utility was positively correlated with the amount of goods and services sold. Wrote Dupuit:

> The same merchandise, disguised in different stores under various forms, is often sold at very different prices to the rich, the well-to-do, and the poor. There is the fine, the very-fine, the extra-fine, and the super-fine, which, although drawn from the same barrel, present no real difference other than a better label and a higher price. Why? Because the same thing has a very different utility value for the consumer. If the goods were sold only at an average price, all those who attached less utility than this price would not buy, and thus incur a loss; and the seller would lose because many of his customers would be paying for only a very small part of the utility they receive.[9]

It should be noted that another interesting aspect of Dupuit was his dispute with the French liberals of his day, who saw property rights as justified on the basis of natural law while Dupuit saw them justified primarily on the basis of public utility. Finally, Dupuit has been credited with the first exposition of marginal utility theory. Wrote William Stanley Jevons, in *The Theory of Political Economy*:

> It is the French engineer Dupuit who must probably be credited with the earliest perfect comprehension of the theory of utility. In attempting to frame a precise measure of the utility of public works, he observed that the utility of a commodity not only varies immensely from one individual to another, but that it is also widely different for the same person according to circumstances.[10]

Recall that we previously touched on the German historicist school, which challenged classical economics as being too theoretical and overly focused on deductive reasoning. Let us now shift our attention to the

---

[9]A.J. Dupuit. 1853. *On Utility and Its Measure*, p. 177, as quoted in Ekelund and Hebert, p. 327 .

[10]Preface to the Second Edition (1879).

Austrian school of economics, which formed at least in part in opposition to the historicists. We will initially focus on Carl Menger (1840–1921), Freidrich Wieser (1851–1926), and Eugen Bohm-Bawerk (1851–1914). Later, we will examine the work of subsequent disciples of the Austrian school, including Ludwig von Mises (1881–1973) and Friedrich Hayek (1899–1992).

Carl Menger

Carl Menger published his *Principles of Economics* in 1871. In his introduction to a later printing of that book, F. A. Hayek noted that William Stanley Jevons, Carl Menger, and Léon Walras all apparently independently discovered the marginal utility principle, and that the year 1871 may be regarded as a watershed year for modern economics with both Menger's book and Jevons's *Theory of Political Economy* being published.[11] In particular, Menger advanced the assault on the classical labor theory of value and demonstrated that value is subjective (in large part tied to the opportunity cost associated with alternative trades) in a way that allowed for win–win exchange.

It has been said that capitalism is organized around scarcity, and Menger also noted that to ascribe value to a good for purposes of trade presupposes the good is in some meaningful sense scarce. This was part of the marginalist revolution's response to the paradox of value, which in one popular formulation posited that it is in some sense contradictory for water to be deemed less valuable than diamonds when water is essential to life while diamonds are not. Adam Smith and the classical economists attempted to resolve this paradox via the labor theory of value, which ascribed a fundamental value to goods based on the labor required to produce them. Menger and the other marginalists rejected this use of the labor theory of value and focused instead on the subjective value placed on goods by consumers, which varied based on the quantity of goods available (e.g., you would pay a lot more for the first glass of water if you were thirsty, but much less for the tenth). At least some commentators have criticized this

---

[11]*See* C. Menger. 2007. *Principles of Economics* (Auburn, AL: Ludwig Von Mises Institute), p. 12.

approach for going too far in essentially ignoring production costs and/or derived income.[12]

Menger is also well known for his explanation of the origin of money, which he essentially posits as arising in response to what economists typically refer to as the problem of the double coincidence of wants.[13] Basically, the idea is that an economy that relies on barter makes it very difficult to trade where every party to a proposed exchange doesn't have something the other party desires and values in a way that allows for trading.[14] By introducing a good that is commonly valued and easy to carry, like gold or gems, exchange is facilitated. In other words, if you have a goat you'd like to exchange for a cow but I don't have a cow, I can give you some quantity of gold in exchange for the goat that should allow you to obtain a cow later. Thus, the introduction of money into an economy is essentially organic, and it is not hard to see how it is a relatively short step to the introduction of paper money, which is even easier to carry around than gold.[15] Nevertheless, the question of whether money should be tied to specie, such as gold, remains controversial.

---

[12]*See, e.g., generally*, M. Dobb. 1975. *Theories of Value and Distribution since Adam Smith: Ideology and Economic Theory* (Cambridge, UK: Cambridge University Press).

[13]*See* W.S. Jevons. 1875. *Money and the Mechanism of Exchange* 1.5 (New York, NY: D. Appleton and Company).

> "The first difficulty in barter is to find two persons whose disposable possessions mutually suit each other's wants. There may be many people wanting, and many possessing those things wanted; but to allow of an act of barter, there must be a double coincidence, which will rarely happen. . . . Sellers and purchasers can only be made to fit by the use of some commodity, some *marchandise banale*, as the French call it, which all are willing to receive for a time, so that what is obtained by sale in one case, may be used in purchase in another. This common commodity is called a *medium, of exchange*, because it forms a third or intermediate term in all acts of commerce."

Id.

[14]This may just be a restatement of Aristotle. *See generally*, M. Manning, E. Nier, and J. Schanz. 2009. *The Economics of Large-value Payments and Settlement: Theory and Policy Issues for Central Banks* (Oxford, UK: Oxford University Press).

[15]*Compare* M. Manning, E. Nier, and J. Schanz. 2009. *The Economics of Large-value Payments and Settlement: Theory and Policy Issues for Central Banks* (Oxford, UK: Oxford University Press) (noting Cartelist theory of money as being rooted in the power and credibility of the issuer).

Friedrich von Weiser

Friedrich von Weiser (1851–1926) advanced the work of Menger, among other things coining the phrase "marginal utility." Weiser is best known for his works *Natural Value* (1889) and *Social Economics* (1914). Although Weiser is likely best understood as a proponent of a truly competitive, entrepreneurial system as best enhancing economic growth, he also wrote about the limits of such a system. For example, he noted one potentially distorting impact of unequal income distribution:

> Instead of the things that would be more useful, there are [produced] things that pay better. The greater the difference in wealth, the more striking are the anomalies of production. The economy provides luxury to the capricious and greedy, while it is deaf to the needs of the miserable and poor. It is therefore the distribution of wealth that decides what will be produced, and leads to a consumer of a more anti-economic variety: a consumer wastes on unnecessary, guilty enjoyment that which could have served to heal the wounds of poverty.[16]

It is noteworthy that von Weiser's analysis does not reflect an appreciation of the possibility that a broader distribution will positively impact not only what, but also how much more, is produced in the aggregate.

Eugen Bohm-Bawerk

Relatedly, Eugen Bohm-Bawerk (1851–1914), generally described as the third founder of Austrian economics, argued that market exchange will continue to push prices toward an equilibrium where supply and demand meet by, among other things, excluding buyers who are not willing or, perhaps more importantly, not able to pay the price that clears the market and by drawing sellers to markets where demand is unmet till there is no room left for additional sellers to enter the market profitably. The price at which this equilibrium is reached is determined by the coming together

---

[16]Friedrich von Wieser.1893. *Natural Value* (London, UK: Macmillan), p. 58.

of the marginal pairs of buyers and sellers. Unmet demand remains, but no one has an incentive to satisfy this demand because, by definition, this cannot be done profitably (or at least not without incurring an irrational opportunity cost). Unlike the dominant Marshallian view (more to come on that later), the Austrian view of Bohm-Bawerk stressed the finite number of traders, which produce what might be referred to as staccato, as opposed to smooth, supply and demand functions.

Bohm-Bawerk's magnum opus is *Capital and Interest*, a collection of three volumes: *History and Critique of Interest Theories* (1884), *Positive Theory of Capital* (1889), and *Further Essays on Capital and Interest* (1914). He is well known for highlighting the tension created by "roundabout" methods of production, which forego immediate rewards available via application of existing methods of production (e.g., wading into the water to catch fish with a spear) in order to reap greater gains later after having invested in creating better methods (e.g., a boat and net to allow one to fish more productively in better spots). Because people typically value the current consumption of goods higher than later consumption of the same good, the delay in consumption must be compensated and Bohm-Bawerk identified this as the justification for interest. This led to his refutation of Marx's exploitation theory of capitalism because, as Bohm-Bawerk saw it, rather than expropriating labor value in the form of profit the capitalist was earning interest on the advances he made to workers in the form of wages that sustained them while they produced the products that would ultimately generate value for them. As will be discussed below, the notion that earners must defer from consumption to facilitate investment rests on the questionable assumption that there is no important distinction between real savings and financial savings. It also assumes that the investors have current unmet needs and desires to defer.

William Stanley Jevons

Shifting our attention to the evolution of neoclassical microeconomics in England and America brings us to William Stanley Jevons (1835–1882) who is best known for his *Theory of Political Economy* (1871) and his insights into utility theory, including his independent exposition of marginal utility as well as the equimarginal principle, which is explained in more detail below. Together with Carl Menger and Léon Walras, Jevons is considered one of the three cofounders of marginal utility analysis.

Jevons clearly identifies utility maximization with pleasure maximization and eschews any value judgments of individual preferences:

> Pleasure and pain are undoubtedly the ultimate objects of the Calculus of Economics. To satisfy our wants to the utmost with the least effort—to procure the greatest amount of what is desirable at the expense of the least that is undesirable—in other words, to maximise pleasure, is the problem of Economics. . . . Whatever can produce pleasure or prevent pain may possess utility. . . . but we must beware of restricting the meaning of the word by any moral considerations. Anything which an individual is found to desire and to labour for must be assumed to possess for him utility. In the science of Economics we treat men not as they ought to be, but as they are.[17]

Thus, Jevons minimized the role of intrinsic value more substantially than any of his predecessors and rather highlighted the role of individual preferences (utility) in determining value. However, it is worth noting that Jevons ultimately became a critic of *laissez-faire* policies, favoring a utilitarian analysis to guide our policies:

> While population grows more numerous and dense, while industry becomes more complex and interdependent, as we travel faster and make use of more intense forces, we shall necessarily need more legislative supervision. If such a thing is possible, we need a new branch of political and statistical science which shall carefully investigate the limits to the *laissez-faire* principle, and show where we want greater freedom and where less. . . . Instead of one

---

[17] *Theory*, at III.1 & 2. *But cf. id.* ("A very large part of the labour of any community is spent upon the production of the ordinary necessaries and conveniences of life, such as food, clothing, buildings, utensils, furniture, ornaments, etc.; and the aggregate of these things, therefore, is the immediate object of our attention.").

dictum, *laissez-faire, laissez-passer*, we must have at least one science, one new branch of the old political economy.[18]

The equimarginal principle mentioned above extends marginal utility analysis to competing commodities, which is to say it produces a rule whereby a consumer faced with a limited supply of income should be expected to allocate that income among competing goods in such a way as to maximize overall utility. In order to ensure that there is no utility "left on the table," income should be allocated between products A and B in such a way as to make the utility derived from the next purchase of A equal to that of the next purchase of B.[19]

Jevons also sought to explain worker behavior (i.e., labor supply) as a function of utility:

A free labourer endures the irksomeness of work because the pleasure he expects to receive, or the pain he expects to ward off, by means of the produce, exceeds the pain of exertion. When labour itself is a worse evil than that which it saves him from, there can be no motive for further exertion, and he ceases. Therefore he will cease to labour just at the point when the pain becomes equal to the corresponding pleasure gained. . . .[20]

The implications of this perspective may be debated. It rests on the questionable assumption that an economy like that of the United States can be analyzed as though it is at or near full capacity. In addition, Steven Pressman has noted that utility theory, as opposed to the classical theory of wages, makes unemployment essentially a simple choice of preferring leisure.[21]

---

[18]1876. "The Future of Political Economy," *The Fortnightly Review 20*, no. 629.

[19]Hermann Heinrich Gossen (1810–1858) is frequently given credit for this insight, which can be described as "Gossen's Second Law." Gossen has also been given credit for introducing graphical analysis into economics.

[20]W.S. Jevons. 1871. "Chapter V: Theory of Labour." *The Theory of Political Economy*. London, UK: Macmillan and Co.

[21]S. Pressman. 2013. *Fifty Major Economists,* 3rd ed., (London, UK: Routledge), p. 79.

Despite all the foregoing, a review of Jevons would likely be incomplete without noting that he displayed a great admiration for statistical investigation, which led him at one point to conclude financial crises could be predicted via sunspot patterns, for which he was admittedly roundly ridiculed. Wrote Jevons in *The Solar Period and the Price of Corn* (1875):

> If the planets govern the sun, and the sun governs the vintages and harvests, and thus the prices of food and raw materials and the state of the money market, it follows that the configurations of the planets may prove to be the remote causes of the greatest commercial disasters.[22]

John Bates Clark

John Bates Clark (1847–1938), author of *The Distribution of Wealth* (1899), is often cited as the American spearhead of the marginalist revolution. Clark expanded Ricardo's rent principle, whereby the value of land is determined by the last unit in cultivation, to all factors of production, including labor:

> It is by assuming perfectly free competition among employers that we are able to say that the man on the intensive margin of an agricultural force of laborers will get, as pay, the value of his product. When such a man offers himself to an employer, he is virtually offering an addition to the farmer's crop. If one farmer will not pay the market price of the additional produce, another will pay it, provided that competition does its work quite perfectly. Friction is, however, always an element to be taken into account; for adjustments like this are not perfect in any society. Our sole present inquiry is, nevertheless, to determine the standard to which wages tend to conform—the standard to which they would conform in a frictionless society. Our answer is that wages conform to the product that is attributable to marginal labor.[23]

---

[22] W.S. Jevons. 1909. *Investigations in Currency & Finance* (London, UK: Macmillan & Co.), p. 185.

[23] *Distribution of Wealth*, pp. 99–100.

As Clark appears to recognize in the foregoing quotation, while the marginal productivity principle clearly marks a valuable contribution in the history of economic thought, it leaves a number of factors, characterized amorphously as "friction", out of the equation. Furthermore, Clark was severely criticized for advancing normative conclusions from his theorizing, particularly in response to his assertions that market wages were in some meaningful sense fair.[24]

Alfred Marshall

The foregoing review of economic thinkers from Cournot to Clark has laid the groundwork for a discussion of Alfred Marshall (1842–1924) and Leon Walras (1834–1910), who have been referred to as the co-founders of modern neoclassical economics. We will first examine the contributions of Marshall, who was apparently drawn to the study of economics at least in part by a desire to understand how poverty and inequality arose in society.[25] Marshall was also apparently quite adept at mathematical modeling, but was concerned about overreliance on equations.[26]

While other economists had implied a qualifying "other things being equal" in their proclamations, Marshall shone a particularly bright light on *ceteris paribus* assumptions:

The element of time is a chief cause of those difficulties in economic investigations which make it necessary for man with his limited powers to go step by step; breaking up a complex question, studying one bit at a time, and at last combining his partial solutions into a more or less complete solution of the whole riddle. In breaking it up, he segregates those disturbing causes, whose wanderings happen to be inconvenient, for the time in

---

[24]*See generally*, T.C. Leonard. 2003. "'A Certain Rude Honesty': John Bates Clark as a Pioneering Neoclassical Economist." *History of Political Economy* 35, no. 3, p. 530. (describing Clark's claim as controversial).

[25]*See generally*, A.C. Pigou. 1925. *Memorials of Alfred Marshall.* (London, UK: Macmillan).

[26]*Id.* p. 427.

a pond called *Cæteris Paribus*. The study of some group of tendencies is isolated by the assumption *other things being equal*: the existence of other tendencies is not denied, but their disturbing effect is neglected for a time. The more the issue is thus narrowed, the more exactly can it be handled: but also the less closely does it correspond to real life. Each exact and firm handling of a narrow issue, however, helps towards treating broader issues, in which that narrow issue is contained, more exactly than would otherwise have been possible.[27]

Marshall put a great deal of effort into examining the nature of demand functions, which typically relate quantity produced to price inversely. In fact, an entire strand of demand theory is frequently referred to as "Marshallian." Part of what motivated this focus on demand was a perceived overemphasis on costs-of-production as determinative of price. Furthermore, Marshall highlighted the fact that the amount of money/income/wealth a consumer has impacts competitive equilibrium:

> The larger the amount of a thing that a person has the less, other things being equal (i.e. the purchasing power of money, and the amount of money at his command being equal), will be the price which he will pay for a little more of it: or in other words his marginal demand price for it diminishes. His demand becomes efficient, only when the price which he is willing to offer reaches that at which others are willing to sell. This last sentence reminds us that we have as yet taken no account of changes in the marginal utility of money, or general purchasing power. At one and the same time, a person's material resources being unchanged, the marginal utility of money to him is a fixed quantity, so that the prices he is just willing to pay for two commodities are to one another in the same ratio as the utility of those two commodities. A greater utility will be

---

[27]A. Marshall. 1890. *Principles of Economics* (London: Macmillan and Co.), p. 366.

required to induce him to buy a thing if he is poor than if he is rich. We have seen how the clerk with £100 a year will walk to business in a heavier rain than the clerk with £300 a year. But although the utility, or the benefit, that is measured in the poorer man's mind by twopence is greater than that measured by it in the richer man's mind; yet if the richer man rides a hundred times in the year and the poorer man twenty times, then the utility of the hundredth ride which the richer man is only just induced to take is measured to him by twopence; and the utility of the twentieth ride which the poorer man is only just induced to take is measured to him by twopence. For each of them the marginal utility is measured by twopence; but this marginal utility is greater in the case of the poorer man than in that of the richer. In other words, the richer a man becomes the less is the marginal utility of money to him; every increase in his resources increases the price which he is willing to pay for any given benefit. And in the same way every diminution of his resources increases the marginal utility of money to him, and diminishes the price that he is willing to pay for any benefit.[28]

One of the implications of the foregoing is that it undermines the assumption that price paid equals utility derived. Thus, a consequence of holding the value of money constant is an inevitable over- or underestimation of utility, which has particular implications for the calculation of consumer surplus.

Assuming that a market demand curve tells us how much utility is produced by a commodity, and that this utility can be equated with social satisfaction, Marshall was open to the possibility that government intervention in markets via taxation or the provision of subsidies might be necessary to maximize utility. For example, he noted that under certain conditions the expected loss of consumer surplus likely to result from taxing a particular commodity or industry could theoretically be more than offset by the welfare created by the government's use of the tax revenue.

---

[28] *Principles*, p. 95.

Conversely, the expected added consumer surplus generated by price reductions in response to government subsidies could be outweighed by the cost of the subsidy and therefor merely demonstrating that a subsidy increases consumer surplus vis-à-vis the subsidized commodity or industry does not necessarily make the subsidy social utility maximizing or welfare maximizing. However, in "decreasing cost" industries such as various public utilities, subsidies would maximize welfare. (Decreasing cost industries benefit from lower costs as the industry expands and can be contrasted with increasing cost and constant cost industries.) Throughout all of this, Marshall was careful not to overstate the assumption that price information could be directly translated into social welfare because to do so "assumes that all differences in wealth between the different parties concerned may be neglected."[29] Stated differently, we should not ignore the fact that "the happiness which an additional shilling brings to a poor man is much greater than that which it brings to a rich one."[30] This understanding of interpersonal utility comparisons allows one to argue that, for example, some types of wealth redistribution may increase overall social welfare.

Marshall is also known for expanding our understanding of "externalities," which are social costs created by a producer who is not required to bear them and who thus produces more than would be the case if all relevant costs were taken into account (thus imposing more costs on society). The classic example of this is the factory that spews pollution without accounting for any of the costs incurred by the surrounding community. A "Marshallian" solution to this problem proposed by Marshall's protégé Arthur Pigou (1877–1959) is to tax the producer in such a way as to result in internalization of the relevant costs. However, Ronald Coase (1910–2013) argued that, assuming no bargaining and other transaction costs, government intervention was not necessary to solve this problem. Coase's Theorem, which is set forth in Coase's famous work *The Problem of Social Cost* (1960), posits that so long as property rights are granted in a way that allows for trading in, for example, air quality—again, assuming further no transaction costs (which would distort efficient pricing)—the cost of the externality will be

---

[29] *Principles*, p. 471.

[30] *Id.* at p. 474.

determined and allocated efficiently.[31] Coase's Theorem has been credited with spawning the so-called law and economics movement (more accurately called the law and neoclassical economics movement), which seeks to analyze the impact of different legal rules on the economy.[32] Critiques of this counterfactual approach are myriad. Even assuming zero transaction costs, the assignment of property rights will likely impact the distribution of wealth among the bargainers, which may in turn impact transactions with other people in ways that can negatively impact social welfare.

Finally, Marshall also advanced our understanding of "elasticity," which refers to the degree to which a variable (e.g., demand) responds to changes in another variable (e.g., price). We can say that demand is "perfectly inelastic" if demand for a product stays the same as price fluctuates.

All in all, Marshall sought to ground economic analysis in the realm of science, though he felt economics, as a social science, was more akin to meteorology than physics:

> The laws of economics are to be compared with the laws of the tides, rather than with the simple and exact law of gravitation. For the actions of men are so various and uncertain, that the best statement of tendencies, which we can make in a science of

---

[31]Ronald Coase has also been credited with providing one of the most compelling answers to the question: Why do firms exist if market exchange is so efficient, given that firms typically centralize management? His answer: Transaction costs. Essentially, the cost of going into the market every day to hire, for example, a painter (when you know you will need one most days) exceeds the cost having an employed painter sit around and do nothing occasionally. Another part of Coase's answer revolved around the fact that there are certain people who are simply so good at managing large organizations that the benefit of having them manage a firm exceeds the costs of foregoing organizing a business around spot markets. *See generally,* R.H. Coase. 1937. "The nature of the firm." *Economica* 4, p. 386. *See also* A.A. Alchian, and H. Demsetz. 1972. "Production, information costs, and economic organization." *The American Economic Review* 62, p. 777; M.C. Jensen, and W.H. Meckling. 1976. "Theory of the Firm: Managerial behavior, agency costs and ownership structure." *Journal of Financial Economics*, 3, p. 305.

[32]*See generally,* S.M. Teles. 2010. *The Rise of the Conservative Legal Movement: The Battle for Control of the Law* (Princeton, NJ: Princeton University Press).

human conduct, must needs be inexact and faulty. This might be urged as a reason against making any statements at all on the subject; but that would be almost to abandon life. Life is human conduct, and the thoughts and emotions that grow up around it. By the fundamental impulses of our nature we all—high and low, learned and unlearned—are in our several degrees constantly striving to understand the courses of human action, and to shape them for our purposes, whether selfish or unselfish, whether noble or ignoble. And since we must form to ourselves some notions of the tendencies of human action, our choice is between forming those notions carelessly and forming them carefully. The harder the task, the greater the need for steady patient inquiry; for turning to account the experience, that has been reaped by the more advanced physical sciences; and for framing as best we can well thought-out estimates, or provisional laws, of the tendencies of human action.[33]

Leon Walras

Leon Walras (1834–1910), a contemporary of Marshall and author of *Elements of Pure Economics* (1874), is often contrasted with Marshall. Instead of applying a partial equilibrium analysis to explain pricing by focusing on one or several product markets in isolation, along with some substitutes, Walras advanced a general equilibrium analysis that highlights the interconnectedness of all markets. More impressively, he was able to express this interconnectedness by means of mathematical models that are, however, beyond the scope of this book. Accordingly, he was a critic of identifying marginal utility with demand. One can view the following portion of a previously referenced quotation from Marshall as at least in part responding to Walras's criticism:

The element of time is a chief cause of those difficulties in economic investigations which make it necessary for man with his limited powers to go step by step; breaking up a complex question,

---

[33] *Principles*, pp. 32–33.

studying one bit at a time, and at last combining his partial solutions into a more or less complete solution of the whole riddle.[34]

Arguably, Marshall was more interested in advancing models that could be directly applied, rather than grand schemes that were difficult to apply. On the other hand, Walras's focus on mathematical analysis arguably allowed him to spread his ideas more easily across national boundaries.

Walras has also been noted for highlighting the unique role of the entrepreneur in production, both as a factor distinct from the landlord, laborer, or capitalist and as an agent for attaining equilibrium in market exchange. Furthermore, he was very open about the fact that in order for consumer surplus to be equated to social utility one must take an essentially amoral view of utility. In other words, if someone has a desire for a particular product or service and can afford to pay for it, then many economists will count the satisfaction of that desire as creating utility regardless of whether the thing demanded is a cure for cancer or a vial of poison to murder someone. We also essentially ignore those who can't afford to have their needs or desires satisfied by the self-interested profit-maximization of others. Perhaps because he recognized these limitations of free market exchange, Walras advocated land nationalization as a way to generate revenue to fund government expenditures.[35]

More will be said about the important differences between Marshall's partial and Walras's general equilibrium approaches in Volume II.

Vilfredo Pareto

Vilfredo Pareto (1848–1923) is often linked to Walras, having succeeded Walras as the chair of Political Economy at the University of Lausanne in Switzerland. He is perhaps best known for introducing the concept of Pareto efficiency, which essentially equates optimality with a state

---

[34] *Principles*, p. 366.
[35] *See* J.C. Wood. 1993. *Leon Walras: Critical Assessments* (London UK: Routledge), p. 266. (noting influence of Henry George (1839–1897) on Walras when it came to the latter's thoughts on social reform).

where no one can be made better off without making someone else worse off. The fact that this definition of efficiency leans heavily on the side of maintaining status quo wealth distributions has not been lost on critics. Less widely recognized is the fact that the concept of Pareto optimality assumes an economy operating at full capacity. Pareto was also somewhat of a controversial figure because at least some viewed him as supportive of the rise of the fascist Benito Mussolini.

Francis Ysidro Edgeworth

Francis Ysidro Edgeworth (1845–1926) is credited for applying advanced mathematical techniques to explain how to achieve the best (or "optimal") distribution of resources. To this end, he developed or improved a number of analytical tools used in modern microeconomics, including utility functions, indifference curves, contract curves, and the "Edgeworth Box." His primary focus was on how the benefits of trade or exchange are distributed between individuals and nations. Edgeworth's work helped to shift the attention of economist from the concept of "cardinal utility" developed by Bentham and John Stuart Mill (which required market participants to quantify the benefits derived from goods) to "ordinal utility" (which required consumers to know only whether they preferred one good to another or were rather indifferent as between two goods). With ordinal utility, Edgeworth was able to create indifference curves consisting of lines on a two-dimensional graph representing the locus points at which various quantities of two different goods (such as bottles of wine and pounds of cheese) provide equal utility to a market participant. Conceiving of nations as the sum of individuals within the nation (and the indifference curves of a nation as the summation of all the indifference curves of all the individuals within a nation), an Edgeworth Box can be used to depict the benefits of trade between two nations that each produce the same two goods. Edgeworth concluded that the exact point of optimal production for each nation could not be determined theoretically but was dependent on the relative bargaining position of the two nations, which in turn was influenced by such factors as competition from other exporting nations, the extent of monopolistic production within nations, the extent to which a nation's residents were willing to do without, and nations' relative bargaining acumen.

Edgeworth also made contributions to statistical analysis. Most noteworthy, he developed the concept of the correlation coefficient, which can vary from zero to one to show how closely a change in one variable is tied to a change in another. A coefficient of zero shows that a change in one variable is accompanied by no change in the other, whereas a coefficient of one means that two variables move in unison. Steven Pressman credits Edgeworth as being "one of the five or six most important economists of the early twentieth century."[36]

---

[36]S. Pressman. 2006. *Fifty Major Economists*, 3d ed., (London, UK: Routledge), pp. 94–100. *See also*, S.M Stigler. 1978. "Francis Ysidro Edgeworth, Statistician." *Journal of the Royal Statistical Society* 141, no. 3, pp. 287–322; J. Creedy. 1986. *Edgeworth and the Development of Neoclassical Economics* (Oxford, UK: Blackwell); J.M. Keynes. 1951. *Francis Ysidro Edgeworth (1845–1926)* in *Essays in Biography* (New York: Norton).

CHAPTER 7

American Institutional Economics

Thorstein Veblen

Thorstein Veblen (1857–1929) is known as the founder of "institutional economics."[1] Institutionalism has been identified as the only widely recognized, uniquely American school of economics, though Veblen was to at least some extent influenced by the British historicists, about whom more will be said shortly. Institutionalism pushed back against the static theorizing of neoclassical economic analysis, advancing a more "Darwinian" view, and is considered part of the heterodox strand of economic thought.

As mentioned above, a brief sojourn with the British historicists will help to provide a useful foundation for understanding the Institutionalism of Veblen. Like their German counterparts, the British historicists were critical of the view that static economic laws could be derived from mathematical theorizing and modeling. Rather, they focused on the historically contingent, evolutionary nature of economic systems, which could best be understood via an empirical analysis of the relevant course of history. One of their primary exemplars was Walter Bagehot (1826–1877).

Bagehot was an editor of *The Economist*, which his father-in-law had founded, as well as author of *Lombard Street: A Description of the Money Market* (1873). He challenged the Smith-Ricardo British tradition on three

---

[1] The Reverend Richard Jones is also sometimes regarded as the first institutionalist for his 1831 publication, *An Essay on the Distribution of Wealth and on the Sources of Taxation*, which was critical of Ricardian analysis for not taking a global enough view of economics.

grounds. First, it failed to account for the influence of the unique aspects of British culture on the economic analysis of the British economy brought forth there, and thus overestimated the extent to which the conclusions of this analysis were transferable to other cultures. Second, by ignoring the complexity of human action and decision making, as demonstrated in part by the desire to set off economics as a discipline independant of social context, the resulting conclusions were descriptive of imaginary and fictitious people rather than the actual people that were claimed to be described. Finally, the claimed certainty of practitioners of the tradition was undermined by actual human experience. As to the second point, Bagehot wrote:

> Political Economy deals not with the entire real man as we know him in fact, but with a simpler, imaginary man—a man answering to a pure definition from which all impairing and conflicting elements have been defined away. The abstract man of this science is engrossed with one desire only—the desire of possessing wealth, not of course that there ever was a being who always acted as that desire would dictate, any more than anyone thinks there is in nature a world without friction or entirely elastic planes, but because it is found convenient to isolate the effects of this force from all others. . . . But considered in this simple and practical way, the science of Political Economy becomes useless, because of its immense extent. The whole of a man's nature, and the whole of his circumstances, must be reckoned up and reasoned upon before you can explain his comparative wealth or poverty.[2]

Regarding Veblen, it is perhaps worth noting that he was part of an American culture of pragmatism, which maintained a skeptical view of the highly theoretical perspectives of the classical and neoclassical forms of economic analysis emanating from Europe.[3] He taught at the University of Chicago for twelve years and garnered a reputation as an extremely

[2]W. Bagehot. 1915. *The Works and Life of Walter Bagehot* (London, UK: Longmans, Green, and Co.), vol. 7, pp. 158–59.
[3]*See generally*, L. Menand. 2002. *The Metaphysical Club: A Story of Ideas in America* (New York: Farrar, Straus and Giroux).

powerful social and economic critic, in no small part as a result of his book *Theory of the Leisure Class* (1899). He challenged the neoclassical notion of humans as rational, wealth-maximizing actors, describing the actors in *Theory of the Leisure Class* as driven by an irrational desire for social status (among other things, the book is famous for coining the phrase "conspicuous consumption"). Furthermore, Veblen viewed human decision making as being driven primarily by the material circumstances in which people found themselves, rather than by some form of detached cost–benefit analysis. Veblen was very much influenced by Darwinism and contrasted the evolutionary approach, which emphasized change, with the static views of classical and neoclassical economics.

Perhaps one of Veblen's most interesting criticisms of classical economics involved associating it with what Veblen called an "animistic preconception," which involves a teleological view grounded in faith in some type of deity that guides the lives of humans in a benevolent way, such as Adam Smith's "invisible hand." Veblen contrasted this animistic view, which he viewed as more commonly associated with primitive cultures, with a "matter-of-fact preconception" that viewed events in the physical world "without imputation of personal force or attention"—a view more commonly associated with more advanced scientific societies. Wrote Veblen:

> The animistic preconception enforces the apprehension of phenomena in terms generically identical with the terms of personality or individuality. As a certain modern group of psychologists would say, it imputes to objects and sequences an element of habit and attention similar in kind, though not necessarily in degree, to the like spiritual attitude present in the activities of a personal agent. The matter-of-fact preconception, on the other hand, enforces a handling of facts without imputation of personal force or attention, but with an imputation of mechanical continuity, substantially the preconception which has reached a formulation at the hands of scientists under the name of conservation of energy or persistence of quantity. Some appreciable resort to the latter method of knowledge is unavoidable at any cultural stage, for it is indispensable to all industrial efficiency. All technological

processes and all mechanical contrivances rest, psychologically speaking, on this ground. This habit of thought is a selectively necessary consequence of industrial life, and, indeed, of all human experience in making use of the material means of life. It should therefore follow that, in a general way, the higher the culture, the greater the share of the mechanical preconception in shaping human thought and knowledge, since, in a general way, the stage of culture attained depends on the efficiency of industry.[4]

Veblen argued further that the introduction of the utilitarianism of Bentham and Mill did not alter this critique, because as soon as one equates pecuniary wealth maximization with social optimality one is essentially back to a form of faith in a disembodied market guiding all things in the best possible direction for humanity without regard for any values that cannot be expressed in the setting of self-interested actors being led to satisfy the desires of those who can afford to pay in the context of free-market exchange. Furthermore, there is a concomitant resistance to examining the ways in which the idolizing of pecuniary wealth maximization impacts and alters the very desires that are said to drive supply and demand in a socially optimal and natural way.

The bulk of Veblen's analysis is beyond the scope of this book. He espoused a system wherein the basic human instinct to create drove technological advances that interacted with basic institutions in a way that was dynamic. Reminisent of Plato and Aristotle, he described a growing separation of finance and production, manifesting in the desire to make money trumping the desire to produce goods.[5] He anticipated regulatory capture by business interests. In all of this, he criticized neoclassical utility functions for failing to account for the value of acquisition as satisfying a basic human need to emulate and hopefully surpass the wealth of one's cohorts. Wrote Veblen:

So soon as the possession of property becomes the basis of popular esteem, therefore, it becomes also a requisite to the complacency

---

[4]T. Veblen. 1899. "The Preconceptions of Economic Science," *The Quarterly Journal of Economics* 13, p. 141.

[5]It is worth noting that Veblen was writing in the run-up to the Great Depression.

which we call self-respect. In any community where goods are held in severalty it is necessary, in order to his own peace of mind, that an individual should possess as large a portion of goods as others with whom he is accustomed to class himself; and it is extremely gratifying to possess something more than others. But as fast as a person makes new acquisitions, and becomes accustomed to the resulting new standard of wealth, the new standard forthwith ceases to afford appreciably greater satisfaction than the earlier standard did. The tendency in any case is constantly to make the present pecuniary standard the point of departure for a fresh increase of wealth; and this in turn gives rise to a new standard of sufficiency and a new pecuniary classification of one's self as compared with one's neighbours. So far as concerns the present question, the end sought by accumulation is to rank high in comparison with the rest of the community in point of pecuniary strength. So long as the comparison is distinctly unfavourable to himself, the normal, average individual will live in chronic dissatisfaction with his present lot; and when he has reached what may be called the normal pecuniary standard of the community, or of his class in the community, this chronic dissatisfaction will give place to a restless straining to place a wider and ever-widening pecuniary interval between himself and this average standard. The invidious comparison can never become so favourable to the individual making it that he would not gladly rate himself still higher relatively to his competitors in the struggle for pecuniary reputability.[6]

Just as Marx saw the roots of capitalism's demise as existing within it, so Veblen argued that the productive drive of humans, when filtered through the pecuniary culture, would ultimately lead to a decline in productivity as conspicuous leisure and consumption became associated with wealth.[7] However, where Marx saw resistance forming in the labor class,

---

[6] *Theory*, p. 31.

[7] Veblen also agreed with Marx's conclusion that capitalism inevitably leads to concentration of monopoly power in a way that ultimately undermines the system.

Veblen identified the "engineers"—the ones closest to the production process and who had not abandoned production for profit like the owners of capital—as the best hope for averting decline.

John Kenneth Galbraith

John Kenneth Galbraith (1908–2006) may be described as a third-generation Veblenian Institutionalist, following the second generation of John Roger Commons (1862–1945), Wesley Clair Mitchell (1874–1948), and Clarence Edwin Ayres (1892–1972). He challenged orthodox Marshallian analysis by, among other things, questioning the degree to which competition could be seen to drive production and regulate behavior in the real world as assumed in neoclassical analysis and models. He also famously wrote that income inequality was problematic in a number of ways, including its distorting impact on resource allocation (recall the note earlier in this book qualifying the assertion that demand drives production by pointing out that only the demands of those who can afford to pay will be responded to).[8] In his famous book *The Affluent Society* (1958), he essentially called out orthodox economists for feigning scientific neutrality while ignoring the practical normative implications of models that were being used to advance the banner of *laissez-faire* capitalism.[9] As a matter of positive economics Galbraith also questioned whether demand drove production at all, noting the powerful role of advertising in creating demand and the incentives of those in control of production to manipulate wants (recall Veblen's comments about the human instinct to emulate).

---

[8] *See generally*, K. Galbraith. 1952. *American Capitalism: The Concept of Countervailing Power* (New York: Houghton-Mifflin), pp. 104–05.

[9] P. 147 (noting that economists were deemed incompetent if they expressed concern about the market satisfying demands for fancy cars while others starved). *Compare* P.J. Boettke. 1998. "*Economic Calculation: The Austrian Contribution to Political Economy*," *Advances in Austrian Economics* 5, p. 141 (noting a distinction between efficiency/growth and justice).

CHAPTER 8

Modeling Imperfect Competition

Edward Chamberlin and Joan Robinson

Returning to the discussion of how economists sought to model the functioning of actual markets in the twentieth century, the reader is reminded of the two extreme versions of market reality that had been modeled relatively well up to the Great Depression. Alfred Marshall spent a great deal of time modeling perfect competition, which assumed large numbers of sellers who were unable to impact market prices due to the regulating force of competition, homogenous products, and freedom of entry and exit. At the other end of the spectrum, monopoly models assumed a single firm with exclusive control over production. However, in 1933 Edward H. Chamberlin authored his *Theory of Monopolistic Competition* and Joan Robinson authored her *Economics of Imperfect Competition* to try and close the gap between real markets and those described in the perfect competition and monopoly models.

Chamberlin advanced the concept of "monopolistic competition," which noted both that (1) competitive markets involving many sellers may still permit some monopoly elements via product differentiation and (2) barriers to entry in monopoly markets are never absolute. Thus, there is some element of monopoly pricing power in competitive markets and some element of competitive pressure in monopoly markets. Product differentiation may occur, among other things, via branding, location, or advertising (the next time you are in the toothpaste aisle, compare the variety of toothpastes and prices with the much more limited variety of active ingredients). In fact, under both the model of perfect competition and the monopoly model, advertising should essentially not exist because it should have no impact other than reducing profits.[1] By including product differentiation as a variable to be analyzed in value theory along with price, Chamberlin expanded on standard microeconomic orthodoxy.

One of the debates arising out of the foregoing analysis surrounds the extent to which monopolistic competition, which essentially describes many of the markets we encounter in the United States in the year 2015,[2] results in waste. The argument is that waste is inherent in any market that permits even some monopoly pricing power because producers with such pricing power rarely, if ever, maximize their profit by maximizing production. Thus, to the extent one equates maximum productivity with maximum social utility, there is waste. Chamberlin, however, argued that the variety created by product differentiation was itself a benefit that may well outweigh whatever waste is created via the exercise of monopoly pricing power.

One of Joan Robinson's achievements in her *Economics of Imperfect Competition* was to demonstrate that, contrary to prior analysis by A.C. Pigou, discriminatory pricing (e.g., different prices for movie tickets based on age) could actually result in increased output as compared to single-rate monopoly pricing. This is important in part because U.S. federal law prohibits certain types of price discrimination and views price discrimination as *prima facie* contrary to the public interest. However, despite all its contributions, imperfect competition analysis focused on monopoly power has not overtaken the economics profession, perhaps at least in part because working with imperfect competition is messy while perfect competition models can be attractively elegant.[3]

---

[1]While the perfect competition model assumes wants as given, the existence of advertising suggests producers have the power to create wants, which is consistent with some of Veblen's criticisms of neoclassical economics discussed above.

[2]*See generally*, F. Musgrave and E. Kacapyr. 2012. *AP Microeconomics/Macroeconomics* (New York: Barron's Educational Series), p. 115 (noting that monopolistic competition describes the setting for many U.S. and European firms).

[3]*Compare* Dr. A. Dombret. September, 2014. *The economist and the lamp-post—Lessons from the crisis* (relating joke about an economist who refused to look for his lost wallet outside the circle of light cast by a streetlamp because "it's too dark over there," even though he admitted to having lost his wallet on the other side of the street), available at https://www.bundesbank.de/Redaktion/EN/Reden/2014/2014_09_09_dombret.html.

Frank Knight

The foregoing discussion of imperfect competition provides a good opportunity to mention the work of Frank Knight (1885–1972). Among other things, Knight is known for his work distinguishing risk from uncertainty and assigning the profit derived from making successful decisions in the face of uncertainty to the entrepreneur. Specifically, according to Knight, risk refers to circumstances where there is sufficient data to generate probability estimates of outcomes. Uncertainty, on the other hand, refers to circumstances where there is insufficient data to make probability estimates.

Inasmuch as entrepreneurs making business decisions face both types of circumstances (i.e., risk and uncertainty), and perhaps by definition are the people most commonly making such decisions, they deserve the profits generated as a result of good decision making in this area. On the other hand, one could argue that making decisions in the face of uncertainty is essentially a form of gambling,[4] and one may question the extent to which society should incentivize gambling.[5] However, most people will view successful entrepreneurship as obviously being productive in a way that pure gambling is not. With the aggregate economy in mind, it is important to note that many business decisions requiring an evaluation of risk and uncertainty, consistent with the role of the entrepreneur described above, are also made by corporate executives and other employees. Whether by entrepreneur or corporate agent, the dynamics of such decision making are not well defined and the effect is not easily measured.

It is worthwhile to note here that the uncertainty that Knight was focusing on did not arise because it was impossible to determine outcomes,

---

[4]One might also define gambling as taking on a risk that is known to come with a negative expectation in terms of the most likely return on investment, but also promises a significant "home run" return those times when the investment does pay off.

[5]*Cf.* R. Roberts. April, 2010. *Gambling with Other People's Money: How Perverted Incentives Caused the Financial Crisis* (Arlington, VA: Mercatus Center) (arguing that the financial crisis of 2008 was a result of perverse incentives that made it "easy to gamble with other people's money"), available at http://mercatus.org/publication/gambling-other-peoples-money.

but rather simply because the relevant individuals lacked the information necessary for that task. This should be distinguished from economic thinkers who deny the existence of a certain world that could be discovered if only we had enough information. On this point, William Greer has contrasted the position of Frank Knight with that of John Maynard Keynes (whom we will discuss next).[6]

---

[6] W.B. Greer. 2001. *Ethics and Uncertainty: The Economics of John M. Keynes and Frank H. Knight* (Cheltenham, UK: Edward Elgar), p. 46 (noting that Knight believed in "an immutable, ergodic reality" while Keynes "rejects the axiom of ergodicity"). *See* P. Davidson. 2012. "Is economics a science? Should economics be rigorous?" *Real-World Economics Review*, 59 (discussing ergodic–nonergodic distinction), available at http://www.paecon.net/PAEReview/issue59/Davidson59.pdf.

CHAPTER 9

Keynesian Economics and the Rise and Fall of Samuelson's Neoclassical Keynesian Synthesis

John Maynard Keynes

Continuing with our survey of twentieth-century economic thought brings us to John Maynard Keynes (1883–1946).[1] With Keynes we see a shift from microeconomic analysis back to the macroeconomics of classical economic analysis. However, we also see Keynes challenging one of the bedrock theories of classical economic thought: the quantity theory of money. You may recall that the quantity theory of money states, among other things, that an increase in the money supply will lead to an increase in prices. Furthermore, Say's Law (that supply creates its own demand) implied that unemployment would always be temporary because free markets naturally return to a full employment–full production equilibrium. Keynes, on the other hand, argued that the risk of inflation was subject to many factors other than simply the money supply, and that economic circumstances could exist wherein the benefits of pumping money into the economy greatly outweighed the risk of inflation.

---

[1]Ekelund and Hebert provide interesting biographical background on Keynes. *See* Ekelund and Hebert, pp. 531–32. The vast reach of Keynes's life is beyond the scope of this book. The interested reader is encouraged to look into one of the many biographies, including R.F. Harrod. 1951. *The Life of John Maynard Keynes* (New York: Harcourt), D.E. Moggridge. 1992. *Maynard Keynes: An Economist's Biography* (London, UK: Routledge), and V. Barnett. 2012. *John Maynard Keynes* (London, UK: Routledge).

However, he also noted that monetary policy (i.e., central bank actions such as buying or selling government bonds in the open market to impact the money supply and interest rates) alone would at times be ineffective in spurring production and employment, and thus argued for active use of fiscal tools (i.e., government borrowing, taxing, and spending) to generate the aggregate demand necessary to maximize employment.

In explaining his *General Theory*, Keynes explicitly stated that a major flaw in classical theory is its assumption that decision makers use probabilities to calculate the likelihood of various future events. If classical economic theory is based on the assumption that the future can be predicted with actuarial certainty, and therefore decision makers used probability theory in forecasting future events, then this theory is, in Keynes's view, not applicable to real world, which is full of uncertainty.[2]

As with the brief mention of Paul Samuelson and Milton Friedman, more will be said about Keynes later in this chapter and in Volume II.

Paul Samuelson

Paul Samuelson developed a version of Keynesian economics sometimes referred to as the Neoclassical Synthesis, which has been presented in all major textbooks of economics in the past 60 years. In the 1990s Samuelson admitted that he found Keynes's *General Theory* "unpalatable,"[3] and therefore he (Samuelson) merely assumed that it was the fixity (stickiness) of money wages and prices that was the sole cause of involuntary unemployment. Paul Davidson's critique of this assertion is set forth below.[4]

---

[2]*See* P. Davidson. 2015. *Post Keynesian Theory and Policy: A Realistic Analysis of the Market Oriented Capitalist Economy* (Cheltenham, UK: Edward Elgar), p. 20 (quoting a letter in which Keynes describes classical theory as dominated by "pretty, polite techniques" that avoid the reality of uncertainty).

[3]D.C. Colander and H. Landreth. 1996. *The Coming of Keynesianism to America: Conversations with the Founders of Keynesian Economics* (Cheltenham, UK: Edward Elgar), p. 159.

[4]The brevity of this section in no way conveys the importance of Samuelson, whose work is discussed in many other parts of this book. *See generally*, P.A. Samuelson. 2008. *The Concise Encyclopedia of Economics*, available at http://www.econlib.org/library/Enc/bios/Samuelson.html.

Milton Friedman

Samuelson's misinterpretation of Keynes's views held dominant sway over the Western world from the 1930s to the 1960s. Beginning in the 1970s, however, rapid inflation led to monetarism, which favored giving markets time to clear issues like unemployment rather than risking inflation via governmental deficit spending designed to create jobs. The economic thinker most commonly associated with monetarism is Milton Friedman (1912–2006). The debate continues to the modern day, and we can see it in action particularly around the postcrisis austerity movements in Europe.[5]

Paul Davidson

Paul Davidson (1930–present) is unusual among most economists discussed in this treatise because he originally was trained as a biochemist and taught biochemistry at the University of Pennsylvania Medical School. During the Korean War he was drafted into the U.S. Army and assigned to a biochemical research project. Deeply concerned about matters of economic policy and distributive justice, his work on this project convinced him that continuing to work as a biochemist would not fully allow him to address those concerns. Accordingly, after military service he returned to graduate school to study economics. Nevertheless, by reason of his aptitude for, and training in, the rigors of the natural sciences, Davidson (like Adam Smith) brings to economic analysis an appreciation for, and a grounding in, the scientific method that is arguably lacking in the work of some economists who fail to question their underlying assumptions and fail to square their analytical theory with empirical reality.

With Sidney Weintraub, Davidson cofounded *The Journal of Post Keynesian Economics*. Davidson is internationally recognized as an expert on the work of John Maynard Keynes and was commissioned by Keynes's publisher, Macmillan & Co., to write the 2009 book entitled *John Maynard Keynes* in Macmillan's *Great Thinkers in Economics* series.

---

[5]Milton Friedman has been described as "the twentieth century's most prominent advocate of free markets," and the brevity of this section should only encourage the reader to learn more about this important figure. *See* "M. Friedman". 2008. *The Concise Encyclopedia of Economics* (Indianapolis, IN: Library of Economics and Liberty), available at http://www.econlib.org/library/Enc/bios/Friedman.html. Friedman is also discussed in greater detail in reference to Vol-II.

According to Davidson, the version of Keynesian economics developed by Paul Samuelson is a perversion of the fundamental analysis of the cause of involuntary unemployment in modern, money-using, market-oriented, capitalist economies. It was the stickiness-of-money-wages assumption by Samuelson that, Davidson maintained, aborted Keynes's revolutionary role in the development of economic theory because Samuelson's authoritarian influence on mainstream macroeconomic theory made it impossible for economists to engage in a correct discussion of the economics of Keynes. According to Davidson, the result of Samuelson's misinterpretation of Keynes's theory has resulted in the fact that most economists, even those who call themselves Keynesians and New Keynesians, do not know the fundamental analysis presented by Keynes in his masterpiece *The General Theory of Employment, Interest, and Money*.

Davidson demonstrated that in a chapter of Keynes's *General Theory* entitled *Changes in Money-Wages*, there is an explicit analysis showing that even in an economy with perfectly flexible wages and prices, involuntary unemployment could exist and be sustained as long as the future was uncertain and money contracts were used to organize market transactions. Thus, according to Davidson, Samuelson's statement that Keynes's theory of unemployment required the fixity of wages and prices is wrong.

Keynes's theory of employment specified that every penny spent on produced goods and services created a penny of income for the producers of those goods and services. Accordingly, Benjamin Franklin may have been incorrect when he claimed that "a penny saved is a penny earned." Instead, unemployment is due to the fact that people tend to not spend their entire income on goods and services. Rather, they save a portion of their income in the form of liquid assets. These liquid assets are held in the belief that at any time in the indefinite future they can be converted into money which can be used to meet one's future contractual obligations. In other words, savings in the form of liquid assets is a means of carrying contractual settlement power (i.e., purchasing power) into the future. Thus, according to Davidson a penny saved (i.e., a penny not spent) is a penny that is not earned by workers and business firms who produce the GDP of a nation.

Davidson indicated that in Keynes's *General Theory* analysis, unemployment in a capitalist, money-using, market economy results from the fact that decision makers in the marketplace recognize that the future is uncertain and cannot be reliably predicted. As a result income earners tend to store their unspent income (i.e., savings) in the form of liquid assets, which permit them to carry into the indefinite future the ability to buy unspecified things needed in the future. It is this demand to store current savings in liquid assets that creates the possibility of involuntary unemployment in a market-oriented, money-using economy.

Using the modern version of probability theory, Davidson showed that Keynes's concept of uncertainty was the equivalent of the concept of economic events over time being determined by a nonergodic (i.e., unpredictable) stochastic process.[6] In modern stochastic probability theory, to make a reliable estimation of any characteristic of a specific population, a random sample must be taken from that population. The sample is then statistically analyzed for its mean, standard deviation, and so on. The statistical results of this analysis can then be used to actuarially describe the characteristics of the population being studied. Accordingly, to forecast future market prices and sales characteristics with actuarial certainty, the analysis should draw a sample from the future population of the market and analyze it for the mean and standard deviation. Since drawing a sample from the future is physically impossible, if one assumes that the same probability distribution that governed past and current outcomes will govern future outcomes, then one can use the probability distribution analysis calculated from past and present market data to actuarially forecast the future. This assumption that the same stochastic probability distribution that governs outcomes in the past and present will govern future economic events is called the ergodic axiom.

Keynes simply rejected the implications of this ergodic axiom for economics. Accordingly, for Keynes the concept of uncertainty involves an ontological approach that requires the assumption that economic events are generated by a nonergodic stochastic process so that past probability distributions do not govern future economic outcomes. In other words, there is no evidence existing at any point in time that permits one to actuarially forecast

---

[6]*Cf.* Reinhard Viertl, *Probability and Statistics, Vol-I: Probability Theory Stochastic Processes and Random Fields* (Eolss 2009) 2 (noting that probability is used to describe stochastic uncertainty).

economic future outcomes.[7] Samuelson, on the other hand, has written that the ergodic hypothesis is necessary to make economics a science.[8]

Three Nobel Prize winners in economics have recognized the importance of Davidson's association of uncertainty with nonergodic stochastic processes. After reading Davidson's initial 1982–1983 article on the fallacy of rational expectations,[9] Nobel Laureate Sir John Hicks wrote Davidson a letter dated February 12, 1983, in which he stated: "I have just been reading your RE [rational expectations] paper . . . I do like it very much. . . . You have now rationalized my suspicions and shown me I missed a chance of labeling my own view as nonergodic. One needs a name like that to ram a point home."[10] In a letter dated May 21, 1985, Noble Laureate Robert M. Solow wrote to Davidson, "let me first say that I always admired that article of yours on nonergodic processes and I thought it was right on the button."[11] Furthermore, Nobel Laureate Douglas North explicitly cites Davidson's ergodic–nonergodic analysis in his 2005 book, *Understanding the Process of Economic Change.*[12]

Davidson has shown that Keynes's concept of uncertainty about the future of economic events also differs dramatically from the University of Chicago economist Frank Knight's concept of uncertainty. Knight believed that uncertainty was an epistemological concept. For Knight, uncertainty exists solely because of the inability of humans to calculate the probability of future economic events occurring—even though, as Knight wrote, the future "is certainly knowable to a degree far beyond our actual powers."[13]

---

[7] *Cf.* Matthew Bishop, *Essential Economics: An A to Z Guide* (Bloomberg, 2009) 101 (noting that the efficient market hypothesis can be understood to assert that investors cannot predict stock price movement from one day to the next).

[8] P. Davidson. 2012. "Is Economics a Science? Should Economics be Rigorous?" *Real-World Economics Review* 59, pp. 1–9.

[9] P. Davidson. 1982–1983. "Rational Expectations: A Fallacious foundation for Studying Crucial Decision-Making Processes," *Journal of Post Keynesian Economics* 5, p. 182.

[10] P. Davidson. 2007. *John Maynard Keynes* (London, UK: Palgrave Macmillan), p. 186.

[11] *Id.*

[12] D.C. North. 2005. *Understanding the Process of Economic Change* (Princeton, NJ: Princeton University Press), p. 19.

[13] F. Knight. 1971. *Risk, Uncertainty and Profit* (Chicago: University of Chicago Press), p. 210.

Davidson has also explained that the use of monetary contracts in a market-oriented, capitalist economy is the way decision makers exert some legal control and claim some knowledge of future cash flow outcomes, since they recognize they cannot know and control all future "real" economic outcomes in the uncertain world in which we live. Accordingly, Davidson has argued that in a world where the future is uncertain, market orderliness requires the institution of a market maker to guarantee orderly movements in the future at market prices of all liquid assets. It therefore follows that if the economic system is to avoid financial panics and crises, the maker of monetary policy, the central bank, must be prepared to operate as the market maker of last resort in all important financial markets.

Finally, using Keynes's concept of "user costs," Davidson wrote a path-breaking article, *Problems of the Domestic Oil industry*, that was published in the *American Economic Review*.[14] As a result of this AER publication, when the energy crisis broke out in the 1970s, Davidson was asked 19 times to testify before Congressional committees requiring guidance on energy industry policies. In addition, Davidson has developed a 21st-century proposal, using the principles underlying the "Keynes Plan,"[15] which he calls the International Monetary Clearing Union (IMCU).[16] Davidson argues that if the IMCU proposal was to be adopted by the major economies of the world, then the current inducement for each nation to use exchange rate manipulations, export subsidies, and monetary policies to force its products on another nation in order to improve its balance of payments and export its unemployment would end.

---

[14]P. Davidson. 1963. "Public Policy Problems of the Domestic Crude Oil Industry," *The American Economic Review* 53, p. 85.

[15]The "Keynes Plan" presented at Bretton Woods was designed to encourage international trade and international payments to support the goal of global full employment and make it possible for debtor nations to work their way out of debt. However, the Keynes Plan was vetoed by the U.S. delegation headed by Harry Dexter White. Instead, the International Monetary Fund and the World Bank were created and ratified.

[16]P. Davidson. 2015. *Globalization and an International Monetary Clearing Union*, available at http://itnifa2015.weaconferences.net/wp-content/uploads/sites/4/WEA-ITNFAconference2015-Davidson.pdf.

CHAPTER 10

Other Schools (More Austrian Economics, Public Choice, and Behavioral Economics)

(a) Austrian

Carl Menger (Part 2)

We have previously lumped together the Austrian Carl Menger (1840–1921), the Englishman William Stanley Jevons (1835–1882), and the Frenchman Leon Walras (1834–1910) as some version of the founding fathers of neoclassical marginalism. However, as we now turn our attention to the "modern" Austrian school, it is worth noting some of the ways in which Menger differed from Jevons and Walras. As particularly relevant to our discussion here, while Jevons and Walras focused much of their attention on analyzing pricing mechanisms in perfectly competitive markets (with Jevons taking a partial equilibrium approach while Walras chose the path of general equilibrium), Menger was more interested in understanding real markets, which rarely if ever approached perfect conditions. Among other things, Menger was interested in how institutions formed and impacted exchange and how markets functioned in disequilibrium.[1]

---

[1] It is worth noting that Austrian economics transcends national boundaries. One can trace the lineage from Menger to Ludwig von Mises (1881–1973) and Joseph Schumpeter (1883–1950) in the United States, and from Mises to Friedrich Hayek (1889–1992) in London.

Ekelund and Hebert identify five points of emphasis distinguishing Austrian economics from the mainstream neoclassical analysis.[2] First, while marginalism generally embraces subjectivism as part of its value theory, the Austrian view is "radical" because it (a) broadly encompasses individual differences in terms of knowledge, in addition to personal taste, and (b) views subjectivity as determinative of costs (supply) as well as utility (demand).

Second, "methodological individualism" refers to the Austrians' preference for studying all meaningful economic questions at the level of the individual, regardless of how much the decision making in question appears to be operating on some aggregate, collective basis. As far as the Austrians are concerned, all those seemingly collective decisions ultimately rely on underlying individual decisions. The disregard of the institutional (including legal) environment in which individuals acting as agents operate in making such decisions is considered problematic by many.[3]

Third, the Austrian emphasis on "purposive human action" can perhaps best be understood by contrasting it with the view of Bentham's utilitarianism as basically distilling human actors down to passive pleasure-seekers and pain-avoiders. Austrians, on the other hand, view human actors as capable of choosing a discrete purpose to pursue based on their often imperfect knowledge and expectations. Viewed from this perspective, one can see how adherents of the described form of utilitarianism could be quite comfortable using government regulation to nudge individuals in the direction of behavior thought to maximize overall utility,[4] while the Austrian respect for the individual's freedom to choose their purpose would argue against such measures.

---

[2]Ekelund and Hebert, p. 572.

[3]But see Pierre Garrouste and Stavros Ioannides, *Evolution and Path Dependence in Economic Ideas: Past and Present* (Edward Elgar, 2001) 55 (noting common ground between Austrians and Institutionalists).

[4]*Compare* R.H. Thaler and C.R. Sunstein. 2009. *Nudge: Improving Decisions About Health, Wealth, and Happiness* (New York: Penguin Books).

Fourth, to understand the "causal-genetic" nature of Austrian economics it may be best to again contrast it with what it is not. Whereas mathematical models that seek to define equilibrium in the context of perfect competition may be described as part of a functional analysis (i.e., identifying the conditions necessary to reach some predetermined outcome), a causal-genetic approach is more interested in the reality from which the functional form is derived.[5]

Finally, "methodological essentialism" refers to the emphasis the Austrians place on economics being a social science, rather than a physical science. To Austrians, attempts to fit economics into the methodological norms of the physical sciences are in error, and likely obscure the essence of economic behavior. Because Austrians view market activity as a result of a "unidirectional process" involving human actors making choices with imperfect knowledge, they reject attempts to model and predict behavior using the econometric tools so favored in more mainstream economic analysis.

Ludwig von Mises

An example of some Austrian analysis in action may be found in Ludwig von Mises's theory of money. Recall that the quantity theory of money provided that prices would rise and fall along with the money supply. Beyond that, however, monetary theory had little to say about the value of money. Mises closed the gap between monetary and value theory by applying a number of Austrian analytical techniques. First, he analyzed the problem at the individual rather than the macro level. Second, he applied a temporal perspective. Specifically, Mises postulated that the demand for money today was related to its purchasing power yesterday. He then conducted what was essentially a thought experiment whereby he went back in time all the way to the moment when the medium of exchange had value both as an item of consumption and as a store of value for future transactions (as is the case, for example, with gold). Moving forward from

---

[5]*See* M. Rizzo. 1996. "The Genetic-Causal Tradition and Modern Economic Theory," *Kyklos* 49, no. 3, p. 273.

that point one could return to the present day and understand the value of money essentially like any other useful good. In other words, money is not neutral because, at the very least, money must enter and leave the system via a particular conduit and the person or group initially receiving the infusion of money, for example, benefits as they would upon receiving any other marketable good.[6]

F. A. Hayek

Building on Mises's value theory of money, F. A. Hayek argued that changes in the money supply could distort business cycles. Specifically, Hayek maintained that an increase in the money supply would lower interest rates, thereby shifting investment from the production of consumption goods to capital goods. This would result in a reduction in the prices of consumer goods along with an increase in the price of capital goods. All of this, however, would constitute a distortion of natural price signals leading to economic crashes when markets corrected.

A couple of points are worth making here. First, as opposed to the classical economists, the Austrians viewed changes in the money supply as impacting relative prices. Second, because changes in the money supply would not be spread evenly across individuals, winners and losers would be created and wealth redistributed. Given the emphasis Austrians placed on price signals as driving entrepreneurial decision making, it should come as no surprise that they accordingly typically favor limited monetary intervention by the government. In fact, the related debates between Hayek and Keynes are legendary among economists, though most agree Keynes was roundly perceived to be the winner at the time.[7]

---

[6] *See generally*, T. Polleit. October, 2009. "The Fallacy of the (Super)Neutrality of Money," *Mises Institute*, available at https://mises.org/library/fallacy-superneutrality-money.

[7] *See generally*, N. Wapshott. 2012. *Keynes Hayek: The Clash that Defined Modern Economics* (London, UK: W. W. Norton & Company).

Joseph Schumpeter

While the foregoing might suggest that disruptive business cycles are to be avoided, the third-generation Austrian Joseph Schumpeter argued that the "creative destruction" of entrepreneurial capitalism was the key to economic growth. Rather than focus on the static equilibrium models so favored by many other economists, Schumpeter—in true Austrian fashion—was far more interested in the dynamic process of disequilibrium that marked the path of the entrepreneur. Again, this analysis often lines up with a free-market, deregulatory approach to maximizing economic growth. The undistorted market is seen as the mechanism by which entrepreneurs and others arrive at the best possible decisions in the face of limited knowledge.

Additional Comments on the Austrian School

Recall how Edward Chamberlin and Joan Robinson challenged the orthodox perfect competition model by highlighting various real-world phenomena inconsistent with that theory, such as the proliferation of advertising and the presence of monopoly pricing power. Austrians argued that Chamberlin and Robinson had not gone far enough because they had not challenged the orthodox assumption that one could assume known demand curves if only the right variables were employed. According to the Austrians, it was more realistic to assume demand curves are unknown and need to be discovered through the process of entrepreneurial competition. In other words, advertising is not simply a variable that needs to be plugged into an equation to modify demand curves. Rather, it exists as part of the competitive discovery process. Similarly, monopolists must still compete not only because they have to worry about new entrants (assuming no material barriers to entry), but also because the monopolist must still engage in competitive discovery behavior.[8]

---

[8]For more on this, see I.M. Kirzner. 1973. *Competition and Entrepreneurship* (Chicago: Chicago University Press); I.M. Kirzner. 1985. *The Perils of Regulation: A Market-Process Approach, in Discovery and the Capitalist Process* (Chicago: University of Chicago Press), p. 119.

This tension between the characterization of economic growth as a phenomenon with elements that can be abstracted from social context, studied, and applied like Newtonian physics versus being the result of a discovery process that requires competitive markets to flourish came to a head in the socialist calculation debates between (a) Mises and Hayek on the discovery process side and (b) Oskar Lange, H. D. Dickinson, Abbu Lerner, and others representing the calculation side. Mises arguably started the debate in 1922 by challenging the very notion that socialism was a viable path to prosperity. To Mises, once a state eliminates private property and market pricing, producers are left floundering with no efficient feedback mechanism to guide them. Meanwhile, Lange and others argued planners could mimic the market sufficiently to support growth, while avoiding some of the creative destruction and apparent injustice wrought by free-market capitalism. Suffice it to say, the details of this debate are beyond the scope of this book. However, it is worth noting that the debate continues in some form in the political arena to this very day.

(b) Public Choice Theory

The socialist calculation debate provides a good jumping-off point for our next topic: public choice theory. James M. Buchanan (1919–2013) is considered the founder of modern public choice theory. Among other things, public choice theory applies traditional economic analysis to the supply and demand of public goods and government regulation.

A public good can generally be defined as one which provides nonexcludable benefits (e.g., it is difficult to provide national defense only to those citizens who pay for it), making it difficult to incentivize private producers to supply it. Government, however, can use tax revenue to supply these goods, raising issues regarding the supply and demand of these public goods.

On the demand side, the median-voter model suggests that under a majority rule system voter preferences will not be optimized because the quantity preferred by the median voter will prevail. On the supply side,

Gordon Tullock (1922–2014)[9] and William Niskanen (1933–2011) have made compelling arguments advancing the idea that bureaucrats are best understood as self-interested utility-maximizers like everyone else, and thus should be expected, among other things, to seek to maximize the size, prestige, wealth, and so on of their department (assuming that more directly benefiting themselves via the use of their position might well run afoul of bribery and other laws). Other implications include the existence of a "political business cycle" driven by the use of government power by politicians to influence economic conditions in a way that will maximize the likelihood of reelection, and so on. Finally, one should expect political parties to advance not so much the agenda of their strongest supporters but rather the agenda of the voter at the margin (to the extent doing so does not alienate the strongest supporters).

As for government regulation, public choice theory includes the concepts of rent-seeking and capture. Rent-seeking refers to, for example, the allocation to politicians of a portion of the consumer surplus that would otherwise be available to monopolists in exchange for the receipt of monopoly power via government regulation.[10] Regulatory capture, on the other hand, refers to the tendency of bureaucrats to favor their self-interest in such a way as to open the door for interest groups to trade benefits bestowed on the regulator for favorable regulation.[11] It is worth noting that, while this is similar to the Marxian proposition that capital manipulates the political system to divert benefits to itself, the proposition here includes all interest groups. Thus, not only big business but also

---

[9]Gordon Tullock and James Buchanan coauthored what is widely considered to be a classic work in the area of public choice. J.M. Buchanan and G. Tullock. 1999. *The Calculus of Consent: Logical Foundations of Constitutional Democracy* (Indianapolis, IN: Liberty Fund).

[10]*See, e.g.*, R.A. Posner. August, 1975. "The Social Costs of Monopoly and Regulation," *Journal of Political Economy* 83, pp. 807–27.

[11]*See, e.g.*, G.J. Stigler. Spring, 1971. "The Theory of Economic Regulation," *The Bell Journal of Economics and Management Science 2*, pp. 3–21.

unions and environmental groups (as well as other groups) can capture regulators.[12]

(c) Behavioral Economics

The assumed rational utility-maximizing nature of economic actors, which forms the basis of much neoclassical theorizing, has come under fire from various quarters.[13] The psychologists Daniel Kahneman and Amos Tversky have advanced "prospect theory" to explain how value can vary depending on what the relevant reference points are. For example, the value an individual places on an opportunity to wager on a coin toss such that the individual wins $150 if the coin comes up heads but loses $100 if the coin comes up tails will vary depending on whether the individual makes $30,000 or $5 million per year. In fact, even though the expected value of the wager is positive (and thus a rational value maximizer should arguably always accept the bet), there is also a tendency to value loss avoidance higher than an equivalent gain, which can also lead to results contrary to the predictions of neoclassical models. Obviously, the fact that incomes can change, and thus also the "pain" of losing $100, means that the value of the aforementioned opportunity can vary over time as well.[14]

---

[12]Luigi Zingales adds an interesting twist to the discussion of regulatory capture in *Preventing Economists' Capture*, which can be found in D. Carpenter and D. Moss, ed. (2013). *Preventing Regulatory Capture: Special Interest Influence and How to Limit it* (New York: Cambridge University Press) ("Economists who cater to business interests clearly have a larger set of opportunities."). Cf. G. Stigler. 1982. *The Economist as Preacher*.

[13]*See generally*, J.F. Tomer. 2007. "What is behavioral economics?" *The Journal of Socio-Economics* 36, p. 463.

[14]Part of the challenge faced by those who advocate for modeling economic behavior on the basis of humans as rational value-maximizers is that individuals rarely, if ever, have access to all the information necessary to determine which choice maximizes utility, nor are they always able to digest all the relevant information accurately even when they have access to it. Herbert Simon (1916–2001) won the Nobel Prize in Economics in 1978 for introducing the related concept of "bounded rationality," which is one of the key concepts in behavioral economics.

Happiness theory is aligned with prospect theory in its challenge to rational utility-maximizing as the foundation of human behavior (at least as defined by neoclassical modeling).[15] Happiness theory posits that individual well-being and happiness is not necessarily directly correlated with GDP and pecuniary wealth. For example, Richard Easterlin has argued that one cannot simply assume that society's well-being has been improved when person A buys a Porsche, even if we assume the existence of consumer surplus, because person B may experience a loss due to a decline in relative status.

---

[15]*See* B.S. Frey. 2008. *Happiness: A Revolution in Economics* (Cambridge: MIT Press); R. Layard. 2005. *Happiness: Lessons from a New Science* (London, UK: Penguin Books).

Afterword

Volume II continues this history of economic thought. Chapters 11–12 discuss economics following Keynes through contemporary economics and the Great Recession. Chapters 13–14 provide an executive summary of the history and views and recommendations regarding its practical application.

Index

OTHER TITLES IN OUR BUSINESS LAW COLLECTION

John Wood, General Counsel, Quality Health Ideas, Inc., *Editor*

- *Preventing Litigation: An Early Warning System to Get Big Value out of Big Data* by Nelson E. Brestoff and William H. Inmon
- *Light on Peacemaking: A Guide to Appropriate Dispute Resolution and Mediating Family Conflict* by Thomas DiGrazia
- *Understanding Consumer Bankruptcy: A Guide for Businesses, Managers, and Creditors* by Scott B. Kuperberg
- *Buyer Beware: The Hidden Cost of Labor in an International Merger and Acquisition* by Elvira Medici and Linda J. Spievack

Business Expert Press has over 30 collection in business subjects such as finance, marketing strategy, sustainability, public relations, economics, accounting, corporate communications, and many others. For more information about all our collections, please visit www.businessexpertpress.com/collections.

Business Expert Press is actively seeking collection editors as well as authors. For more information about becoming an BEP author or collection editor, please visit http://www.businessexpertpress.com/author

Announcing the Business Expert Press Digital Library

Concise e-books business students need for classroom and research

This book can also be purchased in an e-book collection by your library as

- a one-time purchase,
- that is owned forever,
- allows for simultaneous readers,
- has no restrictions on printing, and
- can be downloaded as PDFs from within the library community.

Our digital library collections are a great solution to beat the rising cost of textbooks. E-books can be loaded into their course management systems or onto students' e-book readers. The **Business Expert Press** digital libraries are very affordable, with no obligation to buy in future years. For more information, please visit **www.businessexpertpress.com/librarians**. To set up a trial in the United States, please email **sales@businessexpertpress.com**.

www.ingramcontent.com/pod-product-compliance
Lightning Source LLC
Chambersburg PA
CBHW062014200326
41519CB00017B/4799